Great River of the West

Great River of the West

Essays on the Columbia River

Edited by

William L. Lang & Robert C. Carriker

UNIVERSITY OF WASHINGTON PRESS

Seattle and London

in association with the Center for Columbia River History

For Wilsonia Cherry, a great friend
of Columbia River Studies

Library of Congress Cataloging-in-Publication Data
Great river of the West : essays on the Columbia River / edited by
William L. Lang & Robert C. Carriker.
p.   cm.
Includes index.
ISBN 0-295-97777-9 (alk. paper)
1. Columbia River—History.   2. Columbia River—Description and
travel.   3. Columbia River Valley—Antiquities.   I. Lang, William L.
II. Carriker, Robert C., 1940– .
F853.G74   1999
979.7—dc21   99-41255
CIP

Contents

A Resurgent Columbia River: An Introduction
WILLIAM L. LANG AND ROBERT C. CARRIKER
3

What Ever Happened to the
First Peoples of the Columbia?
EUGENE S. HUNN
18

"Dr. McKay's Chinook Address May 11 1892":
A Commemoration in Chinook Jargon of the
First Columbia River Centennial
HENRY ZENK
35

Riverplaces as Sacred Geography:
The Pictographs and Petroglyphs of the
Mid-Columbia River
WILLIAM D. LAYMAN
53

On the Columbia:
The Ruling Presence of This Place
JAMES P. RONDA
76

"This perilous situation between hope and despair":
Meetings along the Great River of the West
PATRICIA NELSON LIMERICK
89

"They have no father, and they will not mind me":
Families and the River

LILLIAN SCHLISSEL

112

Changing Cultural Inventions of the Columbia

RICHARD W. ETULAIN

126

What Has Happened to the Columbia?
A Great River's Fate in the Twentieth Century

WILLIAM L. LANG

144

Contributors
169

Index
171

Great River of the West

Essays on the Columbia River

A Resurgent Columbia River:
An Introduction

The history of writing about the Columbia River is puzzling. Before the 1990s, you could stack the major works on the river in a smallish bookcase. Most of them covered overexposed and romantic topics, such as the explorations of Lewis and Clark, the fur trade, the Oregon Trail, Indian wars, and white pioneer settlements. When the Columbia did figure in those histories, it often served as backdrop to other topics, such as the scene of perilous descents through the Gorge by Oregon Trail migrants or as the causeway for Hudson's Bay Company fur-trapping brigades. Literature on the river's twentieth century history languished even more. Readers could find only a handful of books that described the federalization of the Columbia and even fewer that explained what was happening to fish runs.

It is hard to explain this missing literature, because it is almost impossible to miss the central significance of the Columbia River in the history of the Pacific Northwest. The river dominates more than a dozen ecological regions as it flows 1,210 miles from its source in the Canadian Rockies to the Pacific Ocean. The mainstem gathers water from 259,000 square miles of territory, which incorporates parts of seven states and one Canadian province and the drainages of eleven major tributaries—the Cowlitz, Lewis, Willamette, Deschutes, Snake, Yakima, Spokane, Clark Fork, Wenatchee, Okanagan, and Kootenay rivers. Perhaps more important, the Columbia's influence extends well beyond its enormous drainage basin because of the distribution of hydroelectric power generated by its dams and the economic relationships the Columbia has created for the region throughout the world.

Although the paucity of literature on the Columbia did not constitute a total bibliographic drought, the sudden interest in Columbia River studies during the 1990s rose as quickly as the waters during the river's great 1894 flood. The reasons for this interest in Columbia studies are complex, but there is little question that the environmental condition of the river was at least partly responsible. Beginning in the late 1970s, scientists and managers of federal and state river operations realized that declining fish populations indicated a significant change in the river's natural recuperative power. The decades of increasing industrial, residential, and agricultural development in the basin had produced troubling evidence of environmental deterioration. The principal warning came from the plight of anadromous fish runs on the Columbia and its major tributaries. Publication of Anthony Netboy's *The Columbia River Salmon and Steelhead Trout: Their Fight for Survival* in 1980 had documented in strong language and with passionate purpose the worrisome future that faced salmon in the Columbia River Basin. The fate of salmon soon became nearly synonymous with the condition of the river.[1]

Throughout the 1980s, as river specialists studied conditions on the river and as state legislatures, Congress, and regulatory agencies made new policies, the public became more and more aware that a decades-long neglect of the Columbia's health probably mandated intensive care. Fay Cohen's *Treaties on Trial* in 1982 added to the list of significant river problems the plight and struggle of native peoples to regain their rightful place as fishers on the Columbia. By the early 1990s, hardly a week went by without publication of a major news story about the Columbia's ills or planned remedies. Ironically, this new interest in the Columbia only brushed up against the river's history; the public focused on the future—what could be done to fix the Columbia? The river's past, on the occasions when it was invoked in discussions, became contested, the text of arguments about what activity or what group should accept blame for the Columbia's deteriorating condition.[2]

It took the addition of another kind of stimulant to fire up new historical investigations of the Columbia. In 1992, while the Atlantic world commemorated Columbus's landfall in the West Indies in 1492, groups in the Pacific Northwest observed the bicentennial of major Euroamerican explorations that took place in the region 300 years later: Robert Gray's anchoring in the mouth of the Columbia River, George Vancouver's explorations of Puget Sound, and Alejandro Malaspina's expedition to the North Pacific Coast. As part of the Maritime Bicentennial that included exhibitions and commemorative events in Canada and the United States, the two-year-old Center for Columbia River History sponsored a major conference that focused attention on the history of the Columbia River, from pre-contact to the late twentieth century. Dedicated to the study of the Columbia River Basin, the Center is a regional educational and public history consortium of the Washington State Historical Society, Portland State University, and Washington State University, Vancouver. With funding from the National Endowment for the Humanities, the Center planned and staged a three-day meeting held in Vancouver, Washington, on the north bank of the Columbia.

Conference planners recognized the dearth of modern studies about the river and crafted a program that approached the Columbia's past through several disciplines. Specialists in economic history, social history, anthropology, literature, family studies, art, and linguistics addressed large questions about Columbia River history, with particular emphasis on how human communities have related to the river over time. The essays in this volume are revised versions of selected papers presented at that conference. It is clear from these essays that the river's power extends well beyond measurements of kilowatts generated or fish caught and marketed. As physical force and cultural metaphor, the river flows through communities in ways that affect economic activities, social relationships, political action, artistic expression, and cultural

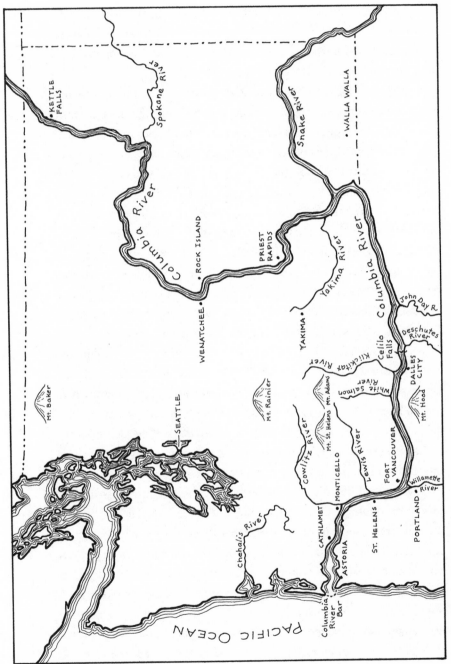

The Columbia River pre-1900 (map by Evelyn Hicks)

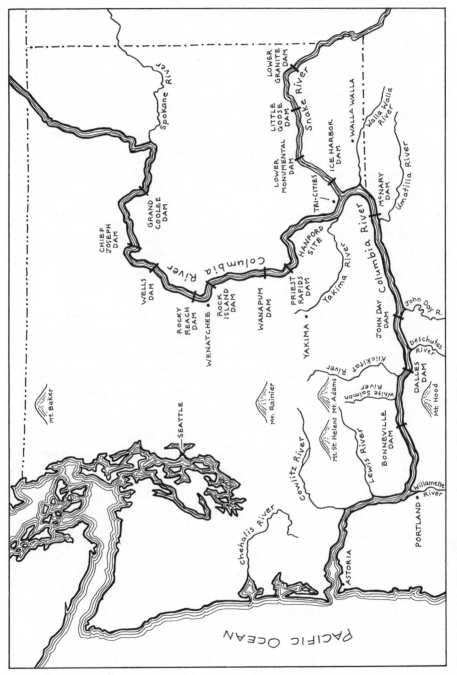

The Columbia River post-1900 (map by Evelyn Hicks)

exchanges. It can be said without exaggeration that little happens in the Columbia's drainage, especially in the late twentieth century, that does not carry the river's mark. Perhaps more importantly, little happens in the basin that does not reflect some measure of the Columbia's history. That is the larger message conveyed by these essays: the river's past is a dynamic presence in our lives.

The Columbia's historical connection with human communities reaches back ten millennia to the early Holocene, after the great Pleistocene floods scraped the topsoil off the Columbia Plateau, flushed millions of acres of water down the Gorge, and floated glacial erratics in icebergs clear up the Willamette River valley. Early archaeological evidence of fishing communities on the Columbia date to 9,000 B.P. Other evidence, including the largest Clovis point found in North America, discovered just west of Wenatchee, Washington, on the Columbia, documents a continual human presence in the basin. Descendants of these populations and other groups who moved into the region hundreds of years ago created cultures that relied on the Columbia for sustenance and meaning. In this volume's opening essay, University of Washington ethnobotanist Eugene Hunn explains how thoroughly the culture of the Columbia's indigenous people embraced the river environment and especially how powerfully central this connection has remained to native culture. It is evident, Hunn argues, in Indian oral literature about the Columbia, in the names of places, in the knowledge of botanical resources, and in the determination to preserve their connections to the landscape expressed by tribal representatives at the 1855 treaty councils. The focus on preservation of place and the right to live in close proximity to the riverine environment continued from early twentieth century court cases to the *Belloni* and *Boldt* decisions in the 1960s and 1970s.

Evidence of the deeper connection between Indian people and the environment appears on the landscape on basalt blocks, canyon walls, and cliffs throughout the Columbia River Basin. For thousands of years, Columbia natives created pictographs and petroglyphs to express their ideas and visions about the world and their place in it. In his essay, William

Layman investigates some of the most remarkable examples of this old-est art on the Columbia Plateau along the upper river near present-day Wenatchee. Layman also tells about the documentation of the images and about the dilemmas that faced dam-builders and native people when river impoundments inundated rock art sites. Although interpretation of the figures and geometric designs is problematic, Layman makes it clear that there is communication in the figures on basalt that spans genera-tions, even millennia. The sites are sacred places, preserving the artistic expressions of some of the region's earliest people and connecting present-day Indians with a spiritual landscape.

In the Columbian world, during the early years of contact between native and non-native people, linguistic barriers created the need to in-vent language to facilitate trade and social communication. The Chinook Jargon, a combination of words and phrases from native and European languages, became the trade patois of the Columbia and much of the Pacific Northwest. Henry Zenk's translation of William McKay's cen-tennial address in Astoria in 1892 underscores both the utility and the limitations of Chinook Jargon, while also emphasizing the ideas and viewpoints that Indian and non-Indian locutors most easily shared. The Jargon, Zenk explains, had fewer than one thousand words, yet it served trading and social interests at fur posts, in treaty talks, and at major trad-ing locations like Celilo Falls. Chinook Jargon brought focus to the meet-ing of people from several cultures.

If the use of Chinook Jargon epitomized the social challenges of the encounter between native and non-native people on the river, the dy-namic importance of the great trade mart in the Gorge—The Dalles–Celilo Falls complex—epitomized the breadth and speed of change that overtook the Indian world on the Columbia. As James Ronda lyrically suggests, it is the perfect place to view what the Columbia River has been to all of the people who have lived in its influence. Ronda recalls the ge-ographic confusions about the "River of the West," including the prove-nance of the term "Oregon" and how Euroamericans found the river and set about inventing it for their own purposes. The Columbia received its name from Robert Gray's vessel, but Ronda argues that the idea of the river is much older and the changes made to it have been the text of relationships between itself and its people.

The overlanders who rushed to Oregon during the 1840s came to the Columbia near The Dalles, where they made a decision to descend the river through the Gorge on rafts and in boats or to snake their way around Mt. Hood on the trail blazed by Samuel Barlow and Joel Palmer in 1845. This way to Oregon, however, was not the only route, as Patricia Limerick reminds us in her description of the maritime approach to the Columbia River. The treacherous bar at the mouth of the Columbia distinguishes it from other great western rivers, and the heroics often invoked in its crossing give the river historical episodes that more than match tales from other great streams. Limerick finds riverine connections between dramatic events, such as the fate of the *Tonquin* in 1811 and William Broughton's standoff against an Indian armada in 1792, as indicative of the Columbia's place as a borderland and as a causeway. It is the ironic that Limerick highlights, and it is in irony that the genuine meaning of the Columbia is often found.

There is in the settling in Oregon and on the Columbia an irony that tests the importance of heroics of migration to the river, whether from The Dalles or from the Pacific. The heroics of settlement, as Lillian Schlissel hauntingly describes, burdened family and women in ways forgotten about or purposefully lost. Abigail Malick's experience in Vancouver is not easily forgotten, and its meaning extends well beyond the boundaries of one family. The Malick story is emblematic of the massive changes that would take place on the Columbia, where a new culture became dominant during the nineteenth century, pushing native people to the margins as it struggled to transfer earlier pioneering experiences to the Pacific Northwest. That culture came from a people in motion, from invaders who brought with them a litany of ideas about environment, cultural hegemony, and economic activity that would re-make the region.

What happened next on the Columbia is understood most forcefully in the range of literature that describes the river and its people. Richard Etulain is the acknowledged master of this field, and his survey of the Columbia's literature—from early discussions of the region by Frances Fuller Victor to the novels of Nard Jones and Craig Lesley—lets us see how the larger culture has dealt with the potential for human achievement on the river and the environmental sacrifice it endured. The latest stage in the literary history of the river, Etulain explains, is what might be called the postindustrial and perhaps postregional expression, which puts the Columbia in a more reflective and global context.

The new literature on the Columbia comes directly from the realization that the river has been an extremely powerful unifying feature in the Pacific Northwest. The federalization of the river, especially through the construction of major engineering works from the mid-1930s to the mid-1970s, is one of the focal points in the volume's concluding essay. The spirit of the Columbia, as understood and expressed through the region's culture, is intertwined with the river's utilitarian role in the human community. Engineers, commercial fishers, and river managers see the Columbia from markedly different angles than Indian fishers, environmentalists, and recreationists do, but there is a shared response to the river that dares us to separate the instrumental from the spiritual, the beautiful from the functional. There is a unity in the effect the Columbia has had on the Pacific Northwest, especially during the twentieth century, even if the consequences to the river have been frighteningly problematic and divisive of human community. There is seeming paradox here—unity creating division—but the reality is found in the range of human responses to the Columbia and in the reluctance of anyone to give up any one response in favor of another.

The essays in this volume underscore the complexity of the relationships between people and their river in the Pacific Northwest. They also pursue the purpose of the Great River of the West conference—to direct new and serious attention to the Columbia. Conversations at the conference spilled out into the hallways and raised dozens of ancillary issues that demanded attention. Some in the audience had come to the conference because they had already begun work on Columbia River topics and wanted to pursue their ideas. William Dietrich's *Northwest Passage: The Great Columbia River* was among the first books to appear in the amaz-

ing outpouring of work on the river during the years after the conference. A Pulitzer Prize–winning science reporter for the *Seattle Times* and
author of *The Final Forest*, Dietrich approached the Columbia as a historical, political, and economic place. His questions about how people
had lived with the river during the last two hundred years led him to conclude that what our industrial civilization has done to the Columbia is
both tragic and desperately in need of revision. Historian Richard White
arrived at a similar conclusion in his brilliant *Organic Machine: The Remaking of the Columbia River*. White takes apart the conventional separation of the "natural" river from the "artificial" by arguing that the
Columbia has been changed so fundamentally that it is in many ways a
new river, one that has been tailored for human needs and human
dreams. In White's book, the Columbia stands as a metaphor for the late
twentieth century's misunderstanding of how human culture is intertwined with the environment.[3]

Engineering radically altered the river, and the largest of the engineering projects on the Columbia was Grand Coulee, the focus of another recent book, Paul Pitzer's *Grand Coulee: Harnessing a Dream*.
Pitzer takes readers deep into the great dam's interior and explains how
engineers solved vexing problems in spanning the Columbia. He also
makes it clear that building Grand Coulee was as much a work of political engineering as it was civil engineering, taking nearly two decades
of bureaucratic and legislative conflict before the federal government
agreed to fund such an enormous structure so removed from population centers. The dam provided much needed employment during the
Depression, but it also sent the lion's share of its power after 1943 to another engineering development on the river—the Hanford Engineering
Works. The controversies—political and historical—about what happened along the banks of the Columbia from 1944 until well into the
1980s are detailed in Michael D'Antonio's *Atomic Harvest*, Michelle Stenjehem Gerber's *On the Home Front: The Cold War Legacy of the Hanford
Nuclear Site*, and John Findlay and Bruce Hevly's edited volume, *The
Atomic West*.[4]

Hanford's history is emblematic of what has taken place on the Columbia during the twentieth century. On the one hand, it is a tale of triumphal science and engineering, one of the nation's remarkable wartime achievements; but on the other hand, it is a dystopian story that includes radionuclide pollution of the river and a legacy of unmeasured danger to human health. The channelization, damming, and impounding of the Columbia had generally received praise for creating new wealth, but the focus on environmental deterioration prodded researchers to ask increasingly critical questions about the engineered river. Some recent studies, such as Blaine Harden's *A River Lost*, have been polemically critical of engineering decisions on the river. Other evaluations of the benefits and casualties of river management, such as Keith Petersen's superb study of the lower Snake River dams, *River of Life, Channel of Death*, and Joseph Cone's *A Common Fate*, have taken a measured look at how relationships between key economic interests and governmental policies led to environmentally disastrous alterations to the river. Yet others, such as Lisa Mighetto and Wes Ebel's *Saving the Salmon*, defend government actions on the Columbia in mitigating the deleterious effects of engineering on anadromous fish, provide extensive documentation, such as Joseph Cone and Sandy Ridlington's sourcebook, *The Northwest Salmon Crisis*, or critique policies, as Joseph Taylor does in *Making Salmon*.[5]

Since the Great River of the West conference in 1992, the humanistic side of the Columbia's recent history has drawn increasing attention in community histories, collected essays, memoirs, and poetry. Evocative treatments of Columbia River environments, with an emphasis on the dimensions of place, are the focus of Kim Stafford's *Having Everything Right*. The insightful and penetrating poetic vision of mid-Columbia Indian poet Elizabeth Woody in *Luminaries of the Humble* reminds readers of the deep cultural connections with the river that continue in the native community regardless of and in reaction to the dislocations modern engineering has forced on river people. Reactions among other ethnic communities on the Columbia are described in Irene Martin's *Legacy and Testament* about the fishing town of Skamakowa on the lower river and in Linda Tamura's *Hood River Issei*, which uses oral history to portray the trials and achievements of Japanese settlers in the Gorge.[6]

Increased interest in the river during the 1990s also drew writers who wanted to experience the Columbia firsthand. Sam McKinney took his boat along the shoreline and among the islands of the lower river in *Reach of Tide, Ring of History*, to find out how small towns prospered and waned in their relationships with the Columbia. Following in the wakes of other river descenders, from David Thompson to G. B. Forde to M. J. Lorraine, Robin Cody took the measure of the full reach of the Columbia in his canoe by paddling from Columbia Lake in British Columbia to Astoria. His *Voyage of a Summer Sun* is part experiential memoir and part commentary on the character of the engineered Columbia. Cody's commentary on the altered riverine environment complemented ecologist Robert Michael Pyle's *Wintergreen*, an open-eyed and critical evaluation of the effects of industrial logging on the lower Columbia.[7]

More than any other topic or force, environmental change has stimulated the renewed interest and writing about the river, but this modern focus has also regenerated interest in some of the traditional subjects of Columbia studies. The incredible exploits and journeys of Nor'Wester David Thompson are related and documented in Jack Nisbet's *Sources of the River* and Barbara Belyea's *Columbia Journals*. Robert Gray's historic sailing into the river has been retold in *Columbia's River* by Richard Nokes and in John Scofield's *Hail, Columbia*. The history of the Columbia District of the Hudson's Bay Company has received modern treatment in Richard Mackie's *Trading Beyond the Mountains* and James Gibson's *The Lifeline of the Oregon Country*, while the trade relationships with Columbia River Indians have been meticulously detailed in Theodore Stern's two-volume study of Fort Nez Perces, *Chiefs and Chief Traders*, and Robert Boyd's *People of The Dalles*.[8]

New works are likely to focus more on the Columbia's future, which is sure to be highly contested, and less on the heroic and distant past. Powerful economic interests will contend for advantageous uses of the river's wealth, while river communities will continue to adjust to changing patterns of development and social investments. How to maintain some balance among competing interests in public decision-making about the Columbia has been the subject of a pile of government studies and reports. Kai Lee, in *Compass and Gyroscope*, proposes some systemic changes that might make decision-making less contentious, but it is clear from recent literature that no easy answers are at hand. Among the collaborative efforts on the river, one stands out as at least partially successful. The Columbia River Gorge National Scenic Area, created in 1986, melded the jurisdictions and interests of federal, county, state, and municipal governments along a 140-mile stretch of spectacularly scenic riverine environments. Carl Abbott, Sy Adler, and Margery Abbott, in *Planning a New West*, interpret the history of this pathbreaking environmental legislation and evaluate its potential as a guide for managing the Columbia's complex environment. The conclusion Abbott and his co-authors reach echoes some results of the Great River of the West conference deliberations that are embedded in this volume. Ignorance of the Columbia's history has contributed to many of the errors in management on the river that have become so evident in the 1990s. Reflection on the history of the Columbia River and its human communities—from ten millennia ago to the present era—is among the best preparations for understanding tomorrow's challenges.[9]

This volume is the result of a collaborative effort. The original grant and program relied on the advice of a remarkable group of scholars and public historians who planned the NEH conference in Vancouver: Sue Armitage, Barbara Allen Bogart, Robert Carriker, Rick Harmon, William L. Lang, Donald Meinig, Laurie Mercier, Keith Petersen, James Ronda, Jennifer Jeffries Thompson, and William Willingham. Additional support in the NEH program came from David Nicandri, William G. Robbins, Eckard Toy, and the participation of scholars who gave presentations in regional conferences during 1992–1993. This book is the better for editorial advice from Julidta Tarver, Managing Editor at University of Washington Press, and it would be far less graceful without Marianne Keddington's perceptive and skillful editing.

William L. Lang
Corbett, Oregon

Robert C. Carriker
Spokane, Washington

NOTES

1. Anthony Netboy, *The Columbia River Salmon and Steelhead Trout: Their Fight for Survival* (Seattle: University of Washington Press, 1980).

2. Fay Cohen, *Treaties on Trial: The Continuing Controversy Over Northwest Indian Fishing Rights* (Seattle: University of Washington Press, 1986).

3. William Dietrich, *Northwest Passage: The Great Columbia River* (Seattle: University of Washington Press, 1997); Richard White, *The Organic Machine: The Remaking of the Columbia River* (New York: Hill & Wang, 1996).

4. Michael D'Antonio, *Atomic Harvest: Hanford and the Lethal Toll of America's Nuclear Arsenal* (New York: Crown Publishers, 1993); Bruce Hevly and John Findlay, eds., *The Atomic West* (Seattle: University of Washington Press, 1999); Michelle Stenjehem Gerber, *On the Home Front: The Cold War Legacy of the Hanford Nuclear Site* (Lincoln: University of Nebraska Press, 1992); Paul Pitzer, *Grand Coulee: Harnessing a Dream* (Pullman: Washington State University Press, 1994).

5. Joseph Cone, *A Common Fate: Endangered Salmon and the People of the Pacific Northwest* (Corvallis: Oregon State University Press, 1997); Joseph Cone and Sandy Ridlington, eds., *The Northwest Salmon Crisis: A Documentary History* (Corvallis: Oregon State University Press, 1997); Blaine Harden, *A River Lost: The Life and Death of the Columbia River* (New York: W. W. Norton, 1996); Lisa Mighetto and Wes Ebel, *Saving the Salmon* (Seattle: Historical Research Associates, 1994); Keith Petersen, *River of Life, Channel of Death: Fish and Dams on the Lower Snake* (Lewiston: Confluence Press, 1995); Joseph Taylor III, *Making Salmon: An Environmental History of the Northwest Fisheries Crisis* (Seattle: University of Washington Press, 1999).

6. Irene Martin, *Legacy and Testament: The Story of the Columbia River Gillnetters* (Pullman: Washington State University Press, 1994); Kim Stafford, *Having Everything Right: Essays of Place* (Seattle: Sasquatch Books, 1997); Linda Tamura, *Hood River Issei* (Urbana: University of Illinois Press, 1993); Elizabeth Woody, *Luminaries of the Humble* (Tucson: University of Arizona Press, 1994).

7. Sam McKinney, *Reach of Tide, Ring of History* (Portland: Oregon Historical Society Press, 1987); Robin Cody, *Voyage of a Summer Sun* (New York: Alfred A. Knopf, 1995); Robert Michael Pyle, *Wintergreen: Listening to the Land's Heart* (Boston: Houghton Mifflin, 1996).

8. Barbara Belyea, *Columbia Journals: David Thompson* (Montreal: McGill-Queen's University Press, 1994); James Gibson, *The Lifeline of the Oregon Country: The Fraser-Columbia Brigade System, 1811–47* (Vancouver: University of British Columbia Press, 1997); Richard Somerset Mackie, *Trading Beyond the*

Mountains (Vancouver: University of British Columbia Press, 1997); Jack Nisbet, *Sources of the River: Tracking David Thompson Across Western North America* (Seattle: Sasquatch Books, 1994); J. Richard Nokes, *Columbia's River: The Voyages of Robert Gray, 1878–1793* (Tacoma: Washington State Historical Society, 1992); John Scofield, *Hail, Columbia: Robert Gray, John Kendrick and the Pacific Fur Trade* (Portland: Oregon Historical Society Press, 1993); Theodore Stern, *Chiefs and Chief Traders* (Corvallis: Oregon State University Press, 1993); Robert Boyd, *People of The Dalles: The Indians of Wascopum Mission* (Lincoln: University of Nebraska Press, 1996).

9. Carl Abbott, Sy Adler, and Margery Post Abbott, *Planning a New West: The Columbia River Gorge National Scenic Area* (Corvallis: Oregon State University Press, 1997); Kai Lee, *Compass and Gyroscope: Integrating Science and Politics for the Environment* (Washington, D.C.: Island Press, 1993).

What Ever Happened to the
First Peoples of the Columbia?

BY EUGENE S. HUNN

The First Peoples of the Big River, of Nch'i-Wána—the Columbia as we know it today—live on the river still. They call it home. They come together each year in April at Celilo, Priest Rapids, and Rock Creek to thank the Creator for the sacred foods—salmon, bitterroot, Indian celeries, huckleberries, and water—that still sustain their spirit; and they clean the graves of their ancestors each Memorial Day—those graves not drowned beneath the dams, that is—returning to the old cemeteries that overlook the river. These First Peoples have their own history to tell, a continuing saga, a contemporary history that is poorly known beyond their own communities. I will try to sketch that history for you, relying on my reading of the documentary record and on what Columbia River Indians have taught me of these matters. It is a dynamic history, tragic and inspiring by turns.

The First Peoples of the Columbia are the direct descendants of the men and women whom Lewis and Clark and David Thompson encountered on their pioneering journeys of exploration as the nineteenth century opened. The First Peoples greeted these aliens—these *shuyapu*, as whites are known in Indian—peaceably, but with a mix of fear and anticipation. They had heard rumors and prophecies of their coming, and they had heard of the whites' great material wealth, of their pale skin, of their magic book. They helped these first explorers in many ways. Without the Indians' forbearance and the generous gifts of fish, of root-cakes, and of advice and information about the road ahead, the explorers would likely not have returned to the East to tell their tales, to publish the journals on which we now rely for a glimpse into an independent Indian way of life.

The First Peoples spoke Salishan, Sahaptian, and Chinookan languages, languages as disparate as English, Hindi, Turkish, and Japanese. These languages found subtlety and power in the orations of chiefs and the sacred storytelling by the elders of Coyote's great doings at the close of the Myth Age. Without writing, these Indians nevertheless faithfully transmitted ten thousand years of accumulated knowledge and insight through the generations. Some elders still tell these stories to a new generation of Indian children, and the quiet eloquence of chiefs still guides council deliberations. In January 1992, I was invited to a meeting at Celilo of the Columbia River Indian people, an informally constituted council led by Rock Creek, Klickitat, and Celilo chiefs. There was no formal agenda, but a number of critical issues were before them, such as a new education program for the children of Celilo and how to respond to the federal government's latest *in lieu* fishing site proposals. A point of contention was their relationship as the *original* Columbia River peoples to the established tribal governments at Yakama and Warm Springs reservations, governments that claim to represent their interests. Chief Howard Jim presided. All present were urged to speak their minds—or, in the native idiom, their hearts. Those in command of the Indian language spoke in Sahaptin, which was then translated for those who could not fully understand what was said. The people of Celilo have a lot of worrisome problems. Their lives are not easy, and they feel a heavy sense of loss when they speak of how things used to be when the Columbia River was theirs alone. They insist the river is still theirs.

Where should we begin with the First Peoples' story? Perhaps with Luther Cressman's discovery of a basalt knife embedded 200 feet above the present level of the Columbia River in gravels of the glacial Lake Missoula flood. This flood carved the Grand Coulee and scraped the channeled scablands to bedrock. It was set loose perhaps 12,800 to 15,000 years ago. The great lake, impounded by a tongue of the Cordilleran ice cap in what is now western Montana, broke loose in one great sweep across the Columbia Basin.[1] Was the man who formed the knife swept off with that flood?

Cressman was also involved with salvage excavations at Fivemile Rapids before the waters rose in 1957, impounded by The Dalles Dam. Such salvage operations have been the norm for archaeological research along the mid-Columbia, one step ahead of progress. Cressman found a record of intensive salmon fishing at the rapids dating to 10,000 years ago—including the use of gill nets, suggested by the presence of grooved stone weights that may have been used to hold the nets in position. During subsequent millennia, styles of tool manufacture changed as the climate first grew warmer and then stabilized several millennia ago, closely approximating present-day conditions. About that time, the bow and arrow supplanted the *atlatl* as the hunting weapon of choice. The indigenous population no doubt increased gradually over those ten thousand years, but remained in balance with the foods the earth offered.

Were the first occupants of these Columbia River archaeological sites the ancestors of Howard Jim and his people? This issue has been front-page news since the discovery of the fine Clovis points in an East Wenatchee orchard in 1989. Should modern Indians claim hereditary rights to these ancient artifacts? The languages spoken by the Clovis hunters would not have been intelligible to present-day Sahaptin or Salishan speakers, just as we could not have understood the speech of Medieval England, but cultural continuity is undeniable through four hundred generations of Columbia River Indian people.

From the First Peoples' perspective, of course, Indians have always been on the Columbia River, at least since the great traveler Coyote—

known as Spilyay on the middle Columbia—prepared the world for their coming, bringing to a close the Age of Myth. These stories, told only in winter, are still told in a few fortunate families. They tell how Coyote made Celilo Falls, releasing the salmon trapped below the Swallow Sisters' dam. He tricked them by disguising himself as a baby strapped to a cradle board, abandoned to the river's current and rafted up against their dam. They took him in, and he stole the opportunity to dig channels through their dam while they were off in the hills gathering roots. Until those channels were flooded by The Dalles Dam, salmon ran up them past a gauntlet of Indian fishermen. Coyote's cradle board could be seen at the lip of Celilo Falls on the Washington side, turned to stone, until it was blasted away to make room for a footing for a railroad bridge. The mythical cradle board and the rock, called *sk'in* in Sahaptin, gave a name to the large north bank village at the foot of Celilo Falls, where Lewis and Clark recorded seventeen lodges of Indians on October 22, 1805.

A short distance up the river from Celilo Falls at the head of Miller Island—as we call it—is a deep hole at the foot of a steep bank on the Washington shore. That is where Naysh-hla, the Swallowing Monster, lived, devouring people. The monster swallowed Grizzly Bear, Cougar, and Rattlesnake, but it met its match when it swallowed Coyote. Coyote built a fire beneath the monster's heart and cut it down, feeding the monster's fat to the hungry people trapped inside. You can still see the groove in the hillside where Coyote was dragged down into the monster's maw. Pieces of the monster were scattered over the surrounding terrain, giving rise to the many Indian peoples who would soon occupy the land. Columbia River elders say they were put on this earth by the Creator and were given the Sacred Law by Coyote. They have been told this by their grandparents before them. But this is not what we style "history."

Just on the "other side of history"—that is, just on the other side of *written* history—a strange animal appears on the scene, a beast the size of an elk but, like the dog, a "pet." Today, the horse is called *k'usi* in Sahaptin and a dog is *k'usi-k'usi*, "little horse." At first, horses were treated as curiosities, but they soon became an integral part of the Plateau Indian way of life, much as the automobile has captured the imagination and restructured the lives of modern Americans. The Horse Heaven Hills above the sere, stark landscape east of The Dalles came alive with horses. A Sahaptin legend recorded by Lucullus McWhorter attributes the phenomenal spread of horses in the Columbia interior to the mating of a stallion from somewhere to the east with a local girl, the daughter of a chief. They emerged with their offspring from a lake, perhaps the same lake that modern elders locate at Roosevelt, Washington, where mysterious dogs emerge at night to leave tracks on its shore.[2] Local tribes still protect their wild horse herds, though the great herds of the Horse Heaven Hills and elsewhere in the Plateau have been exterminated to make room for ranches and farms. It is ironic that Spanish horses have now become a prime symbol of Indian tradition.

Regardless of where Plateau Indian horses originated—whether from fleeing Spanish colonists on the Rio Grande or from the depth of a magic lake—the cultural transformation they wrought on the Plateau was indigenous in inspiration. Horses fit the Plateau way of life like a glove. In the open country east of the Cascades, horses thrived on the wild bunch grasses, required little special attention, yet multiplied a person's wealth and status as well as enhancing mobility. These people were accustomed to a seasonal round that took families each year over hundreds of miles of trail. They traveled from their winter home villages on the Columbia to nearby early spring root camps, then to gatherings at major fisheries for the spring salmon runs, and then high into the nearest mountains for roots to put away for the next winter. In early summer, they joined hundreds of families at the camas meadows, then climbed higher to the huckleberry camps where the hunting was good before returning to the river for the last fall fishing. Then they headed back home to rebuild their winter lodges.

Horses also brought less sanguine changes in their wake. Mounted raiding parties from the southeast might unexpectedly attack a Columbia River Indian village or camp, killing the men and carrying off the women and children into slavery as war captives. When Lewis and Clark asked about the concentration of villages on the north bank of the Columbia or on islands in the river, they were informed that it was a defense against "Snake Indian" raids. Columbia River Indians returned the favor, raiding Paiute camps far south of normal seasonal haunts. Mounted intertribal parties traveled east across the Continental Divide led by Flathead and Nez Perce warriors, dodging Blackfoot Indian parties to pursue the great bison herds. The motive for the trips was apparently not primarily to acquire meat, though dried meat was sometimes packed home, but rather to obtain valuable bison hides and, one suspects, for the thrill of it. By the 1830s, The Dalles was notorious as a slave market.

One significant consequence of the enhanced mobility was an expansion of social horizons. It seems likely that Plateau Indians first learned of white people from bison hunting parties who had heard about the fur trappers and traders from their Plains Indian allies. Perhaps one such hunting party came home with smallpox, unleashing it on their unsuspecting kin. An epidemic on the Plains in 1782 may have been the source of the first documented smallpox epidemic on the Columbia River, though the Northwest Indians may have been infected a few years earlier from coastal trading ships.

In 1492, Christopher Columbus had set in motion a bold experiment in human contact, which precipitated a biological exchange of unprecedented magnitude. Historian Arthur Crosby has detailed the global impact of the exchange of new crops and domesticated animals that followed hard on Columbus's first voyage. The exchange was roughly balanced. The New World got Old World wheat, rice, sugar cane, coffee, chickens, beef cattle, sheep, and horses. The Old World adopted New World maize, potatoes, sweet potatoes, cassava, peanuts, black beans, chili peppers, and tobacco. But Crosby also documents the more sinister biological exchange of lethal pathogens. This exchange was grossly unequal. The New World was infected by Old World scourges such as smallpox, malaria, yellow fever, measles, whooping cough, scarlet fever, plague, influenzas, and gonorrhea. In return, the Old World received— it is believed—just one new epidemic malady, syphilis, which first broke out in Italy in 1493.[3] Syphilis was the AIDS of its day and age, yet the effects of that disease in Europe, Asia, and Africa can scarcely be compared to the devastation brought down on native America by the Old World epidemic diseases.

Why such a disproportionate exchange? The Old World had passed the Neolithic transition three millennia before the New World peoples of Mexico and Peru, and the dense urban masses of medieval cities had provided a rich soil for the evolution of deadly epidemic disease agents. Because the New World was too young a population to have produced such pathogens, Native Americans had neither a genetic nor a physiological resistance to the diseases. As a consequence, Columbia River Indians witnessed the distressing situation of new diseases killing their people mercilessly but having little or no effect on the white people who had come to live among them. The Indians were quick to draw a reasonable conclusion: the diseases had been brought by whites for the purpose of destroying them.

Smallpox was one of the worst killers. The first pandemic in the New World broke out in Hispaniola in 1519. It swept Cortes to power in Mexico and marched ahead of Pizarro into the Inca realm, rendering that great empire impotent against the triumphant conqueror. Did that great epidemic also reach into the Northwest? Some archaeologists believe that sites near Chief Joseph Dam in present-day Washington hold evidence of a sharp decline in population at about that time. The earliest positive evidence of smallpox on the river dates to about 1780, when the pockmarked middle-aged Indians seen by Lewis and Clark on the Lower Columbia probably contracted the disease. There are somewhat later accounts for the Nez Perce. It is estimated that a "virgin soil" epidemic of smallpox will kill an average of 30 percent of the affected population before it runs its course. The survivors have a hard-won immunity, but the next generation may suffer another outbreak, feeding on the young people born since the last epidemic.

The second epidemic on the Columbia came in 1801 and coincided with a heavy rain of ash from Mount St. Helens. The two events inspired eschatological prophecies by Plateau seers who predicted the coming of the whites and the end of the world. One Spokane prophet's words from that time were recorded in 1844 by members of the Wilkes Expedition: "Soon there will come from the rising sun a different kind of man from any you have yet seen, who will bring with them a book and will teach you everything, and after that the world will fall to pieces."[4] Lewis and Clark arrived soon after the epidemic hit. They were followed in short order by Astorians and Nor'Westers competing for control of the globe-girdling fur trade. As early as 1811, Columbia River Indians at The Dalles confronted David Thompson: "When you passed going down to the sea [the month before], we were all strong in life, but what is this we hear . . . , is it true that the white men . . . have brought with them the Small Pox to destroy us?"[5]

Disease is more than a malfunction of the body. Disease calls into question one's right to live. It infects the victim and the victim's family and community with grave moral doubts. Why me? What have I done to deserve this? Such questions are only natural. The belief that disease is sent as punishment or in retribution or that it is induced by hostile foes is widely shared by human cultures. We ourselves—prideful though we are in our advanced medical knowledge—are not immune to such thoughts. Witness the common reaction to the victims of AIDS, a disease that carries with it a strong moral stigma. Imagine, then, how the First Peoples of the Columbia might have felt when stricken with this new array of diseases. In traditional Plateau Indian belief, disease was assumed to be personal. It was a spiritual wound inflicted by a hostile Indian doctor, and the cure required the counterforce of a more powerful Indian doctor allied with the victim. Native doctors—also called shamans because they cured by means of the spirit powers they controlled—were powerless to treat the new diseases. The curative power of faith was broken. Smohalla, a well-known prophet and religious teacher of Priest Rapids, told an army investigator in 1884:

> "Before . . . there was little sickness among us, but since then many of us have died. I have had children and grandchildren, but they are

all dead. My last grandchild, a young woman of 16, died last month. If only her infant son could have lived . . . I labored hard to save them, but my medicine would not work as it used to."[6]

Perhaps the destruction of the Indians was "the will of God," as some whites loudly proclaimed. In November 1847, acting on the belief that "Marcus Whitman many years ago made a long journey to the east [in 1842] to get a bottle of poison for us," a group of Cayuse warriors overwhelmed Whitman's mission near Walla Walla, killing him, his wife Narcissa, and perhaps ten other unfortunate witnesses to the event.[7] Soon, the missions closed, and the great Hudson's Bay Company pulled out of what had by then become United States territory.

The white settlers established in Oregon Territory reacted to the Whitman incident with alarm and hastily organized parties of irregular militia to pursue the murderers. The federal government also responded, directing the army to establish control in the "Indian country" east of the Cascades. Thus the stage was set for the treaty councils of 1855. Governor Isaac Stevens and General Joel Palmer, each in charge of Indian affairs for their respective territories of Washington and Oregon, prepared a careful plan to divest the Indians of the largest part of their land, "to purchase all their country," as Stevens's secretary phrased it.[8] Stevens and Palmer subsequently negotiated ten treaties in the two territories during 1854 and 1855. All were duly ratified by the distant Senate and signed into law by President Buchanan. The treaties, modeled on documents that had proved useful in dealing with Indian tribes on the Missouri, all followed the same outline and used much the same language.

The Yakama treaty begins by naming the signatory parties:

> Articles of agreement and convention made and concluded at the treaty ground . . . by and between Isaac I. Stevens . . . on the part of the United States, and the undersigned head chiefs, chiefs, headmen, and delegates of the . . . confederated tribes and bands of Indians, occupying lands herein after bounded and described . . . *who for the purposes of this treaty* are to be considered as one nation,

under the name of "Yakama," with Kamaiakun as head chief, *on behalf of and acting for* said tribes and bands, and being *duly autho-
rized thereto by them* . . . hereby cede, relinquish, and convey to the
United States all their right, title, and interest in and to the lands
and country occupied and claimed by them, and bounded and described as follows . . . [emphasis added].[9]

Heavy words. Note how a "nation" was invented and a "head chief" appointed—by Governor Stevens, of course. The "head chief" was granted
unprecedented powers, powers that no indigenous leader had ever
claimed or entertained, the power to sell 10 million acres of Mother
Earth on behalf of dozens of autonomous village communities within
the ceded area boundaries. Kamiakan had little to say at the council deliberations and subsequently refused the title Stevens gave him along
with the $500 annuity that came with it. Instead, he took to the field of
war in one last desperate effort to assert the independence of his people.

Though the Yakama, Nez Perce, and Umatilla treaties were duly
"signed" at the Walla Walla Council, the official record of the deliberations clearly indicates the great ambivalence felt by the Indian partici-
pants. For example, the entries for June 7 and 8 read in part as follows:

The Walla Wallas, Cayuses and Umatillas, were understood as con-
senting to the Treaty, though some of the Cayuses did not assent
and seemed much dissatisfied. The Yakimas still held back. June
8th. Friday. Much discussion and agitation among the Indians. The
Cayuse and Walla Wallas retract. Kam-i-ah-kun is understood to
express himself in favor of *some* Treaty, but does not agree directly
to the one proposed.[10]

Then the Nez Perce chief Looking Glass rode into the council fresh from
hunting buffalo in Montana. He cried out: "My people what have you
done? While I was gone you have sold my country. I have come home and
there is not left me a place on which I pitch my lodge."[11]

Lawrence Kip, a lieutenant in the army, attended the council as an observer. His accounts of the speeches of the Indian leaders are more extensive than those in the official record, yet seemingly garbled, unless we are to attribute to the Indian orators an uncharacteristic mental confusion. Young Chief, a Cayuse, is recorded at some length on a theme introduced by the rhetorical question,

> I wonder if the ground ["earth" might be a more faithful translation] has anything to say? I wonder if the ground is listening to what is said? . . . The ground says, "It is the Great Spirit that placed me here . . . the Great Spirit tells me to take care of the Indians, to feed them right. . . ." The Great Spirit said, "You Indians who take care of certain portions of the country should not trade it off."

Young Chief immediately followed these statements with the old caveat, "except you get a fair price."[12]

Governor Stevens went on the attack, chiding the Indian leaders for their reticence and their ambivalence:

> Kamiakin, the great Chief of the Yakimas, has not spoken at all, his people have no voice here today. He is not ashamed to speak? He is not afraid to speak? Then speak out. Owhi [Kamiakin's uncle and Upper Yakima chief] is afraid to [speak] lest God be angry at his selling his land. Owhi, my brother! I do not think God will be angry with you if you do your best for yourself and your children. . . . But Owhi says, his people are not here. Why then did he tell us, come hear our talk? I do not want to be ashamed of him. Owhi has the heart of his people. We expect him to speak out. . . . The treaty will have to be drawn up tonight. . . . The Nez Perces [who, led by Lawyer and having little to lose, were willing to sign] must not be put off any longer. This business must be dispatched.[13]

And so it went. Surely, from the Indian perspective, this contract was not negotiated in good faith. The treaty was written in the legal jargon of a foreign language, with translation of the treaty and accompanying commentary relegated to local mixed-blood settlers, none a native speaker of the several Indian languages represented among the Indians attending the negotiations. With his military escort at the ready in case of trouble, Stevens pushed as hard as he felt he could without driving the chiefs away. Yet, despite the coercive atmosphere of the council, these treaties now stand between the Indian people of the Columbia and their cultural oblivion. The treaty recognized their just claim to the lands and reserved for them and their descendants a tract of land "for [their] exclusive use and benefit." It also guaranteed "the right of taking fish at all usual and accustomed places, *in common with the citizens* of the Territory, . . . together with the privilege of hunting, gathering roots and berries, and pasturing their horses and cattle upon open and unclaimed lands [emphasis added]." [14]

Thus, the treaty embodies a deep ambiguity. On the one hand, the intent of the U.S. government was to confine the Indians to an out-of-the-way, "useless" corner of their traditional territory. As Secretary Doty explained it, the Indians "were to remain upon their Reservation when required, and were in no manner to interfere with the whites when off from it." On the other hand, the treaty affirms the Indians' right to continue their customary and traditional subsistence activities—to harvest fish, game, roots, and berries and to graze their horses and cattle (a new cultural enterprise among them) as before and throughout their traditional lands so long as they did so "in common with citizens," language that specifically excluded the First Peoples until 1924. [15] It is this clause that was the keystone of the Boldt decision in 1974 and the ground on which many modern legal battles are fought.

The existence of Indian reservations is contested for in many Americans, both Indians and non-Indians. Those who oppose reservations see them as little better than concentration camps where Indian people are trapped in vicious cycles of dependency, whether on welfare or on alcohol. Those who hold this view—whether well-meaning or not—oppose treaty rights in the belief that they promote an invidious dual citizenship within the body politic. Those who defend reservations and the treaty rights on which they are most often based—and I count myself among them—see reservations in a different light. They provide a permanent home, a land base, a collective anchor—a fund in trust—for the tribe and its members. In the Indian language, the reservation is known as *timanii tiicham*, "the written earth or land." The natural resources of this remnant of the aboriginal territory continue to feed the people. Managed by and for the tribe as a communal corporation, the land has the potential to provide good jobs to tribal members so that they can live well and support their families *at home*. They need not—as immigrant Americans by and large must—constantly uproot themselves to advance their careers. Family ties remain primary, and the tribes are like very large families, not always happy with one another, but still family.

This ideal of economically self-sufficient, reservation-based tribal societies is far from being the reality for Columbia River Indian people, but it is not a pipe dream either. The Warm Springs tribe reports, for example, that 2,300 people, mostly tribal members, lived within the same 1,000 square miles of their reservation in 1984. Meanwhile, the Confederated Tribes of the Warm Springs Reservation—through its successful forest products and hydropower plants and its hotel resort—provided over fifteen hundred jobs. The 1979 payroll exceeded $13 million, and the tribal corporation was able to return an annual dividend of $2,400 to each tribal member.[16] This is not welfare, any more than a corporate investor's profit share is welfare. At the Yakama reservation, the tribal government is run largely on income from timber sales and grazing leases on reservation lands. With this income, the tribal courts administer justice; a professional tribal police force maintains law and order, and, with joint tribal and federal funding, housing, welfare, health, and educational services are made available to tribal members. Despite continuing poverty and alienation, the reservation land base sustains a unique, indigenous American community that enriches all lives.

Yet, the reservation story is not the only continuing saga of the Columbia's First Peoples. In the aftermath of the treaty councils and the skirmishes that followed, some families resisted the urging of territorial authorities to "remove to, and settle upon" the distant reservations.

Strong knots of Indian families continued to live where they always had—wintering on the Big River at Priest Rapids; at White Bluffs; on the Snake River; down the Columbia at Alderdale, Pine Creek, Roosevelt, Rock Creek, John Day, Maryhill, and Celilo Falls at the villages of Wayam and Sk'in; and in the Columbia River Gorge where they fished the Klick-itat, White Salmon, and Little White Salmon rivers and lived on lands al-lotted to them near their traditional homes.

James Selam, my teacher, is a John Day River elder. He was born at Rock Creek just across from his family's home at Blalock, known as *tawash* in Indian. As a child in the 1920s, he lived in a tule mat house, learned his native dialect of the Sahaptin language, and traveled to the "usual and accustomed" fishing sites his father had inherited at Celilo Falls, until the new highway brought tourists to watch and "foreign" In-dians to crowd in with them as they dipped for salmon. James is not unique. His "brother"—all male cousins are called "brother" in Sahap-tin—Howard Jim, now chief at Celilo, was also raised on the river, steeped in the traditional ways of the people of his home village at Pine Creek. In 1992 there was a plan to dump Seattle's garbage in the hills near his old home, a plan he fought hard against. Other tribal leaders, how-ever, supported the proposed development for its promised economic benefits, valuing them more highly than the sentiment Howard Jim feels for the land near the place where his ancestors are buried.

These recalcitrant Columbia River people have played—and con-tinue to play—a key role in local history. The Boldt decision was handed down in a Tacoma courtroom in a case affecting coastal tribes, but the le-gal precedents on which it was based were to a large extent established by Columbia River Indian litigants, persistent and courageous in defense of their fishing rights. Landmark cases date back to *Yakima Tribe v. Taylor* in 1887, a dispute over access to fishing sites at Celilo Falls. In *U.S. v. Winans*, resolved in 1905, the defendant Winans was ordered to allow In-dians to cross his land to use their traditional and customary sites at Celilo Falls. That decision reached the U.S. Supreme Court on appeal, and the high court affirmed the key "reserved rights doctrine," that is, that all rights not specifically ceded by treaty were reserved by—not granted to—the tribes. The landmark case of *Sohappy v. Smith*—later consolidated as *U.S. v. Oregon*—highlights the determined resistance to government interference in the Indian life on the river by a man who is now a martyr to the cause of Indian rights.[17] David Sohappy, Sr., died in 1991, weakened by strokes he suffered during his five-year imprisonment for his conviction in the notorious salmon-scam case. He and his nephew Richard Sohappy had invited arrest in 1968 as well, to protest attempts by the state of Oregon to regulate Indian fishing. The courts in that case established the "fair and equitable share" principle for the allocation of fishing between treaty Indians and the general public. The Boldt decision interpreted this as a 50 percent share, and it is tragic that the Indians' share may prove in the end to be 50 percent of nothing.

David Sohappy comes from a long-established Wanapam family, at home at Priest Rapids. There the best known of the Plateau prophets, Smohalla, lived during the second half of the nineteenth century. Smohalla was a bitter thorn in the side of Father James Wilbur, long the Indian agent on the Yakama reservation. Wilbur struggled to suppress the "dreamer religion" espoused by Smohalla and other prophets and religious leaders among the Sahaptin Indians. Smohalla called on his people to reject white ways and white work, following the plow. He reputedly said, "You ask me to plow the ground! Shall I take a knife and tear my mother's bosom?"[18] At Priest Rapids today, a century after Smohalla's death, the Wanapam Indian community is growing, new housing has been built, and young people are moving back.

This prophetic religion lives on today at the spiritual center of Plateau Indian life. It is known variously as the Seven-drums, Long-house, or, in Sahaptin, Waashat, the "sacred dance" religion. Services are conducted in the Indian language, and worship focuses on giving thanks to the earth for the sacred Indian foods and the sacred water and on preserving traditional rites marking life's stages—a young girl's first bag of roots or first handmade basket, a boy's first deer, the transfer of an ancestral name to the next generation, or memorials to those who have recently died. Elders raised off-reservation, down on the Columbia River, are frequently called upon as advisers by younger, less knowledgeable religious leaders.

The reservation communities depend on the conservatism of the independent river Indians for guidance and connection to their traditional life, while the reservation lands provide an economic base and legal protection for a threatened way of life. This is what happened to the First Peoples of the Columbia. The People still live. The river is still their home. The river sustains their way of life and waters the roots that hold them to their land. They certainly deserve no less.

NOTES

1. Luther Cressman, *Prehistory of the Far West: Homes of Vanished Peoples* (Salt Lake City: University of Utah Press, 1977), 50.

2. Donald M. Hines, *The Forgotten Tribes: Oral Tales of the Teninos and Adjacent Mid-Columbia River Indian Nations* (Issaquah, Wash.: Great Eagle Publishing, 1991), 88–9.

3. Alfred W. Crosby, Jr., *The Columbia Exchange: Biological and Cultural Consequences of 1492* (Westport, Conn.: Greenwood Press, 1972), 122–64. Robert Boyd has sorted out the local manifestations of this global process in *The Coming of the Spirit of Pestilence: Introduced Infectious Diseases among Northwest Indians, 1775–1875* (Seattle: University of Washington Press, 1999).

4. Charles Wilkes, *Narrative of the United States Exploring Expeditions during the Years 1838–1842*, vol. 4 (Philadelphia: Lea and Blanchard, 1845), 439.

5. Richard Glover, ed., *David Thompson's Narrative, 1784–1812* (Toronto, Ontario: Champlain Society, 1962), 366–7.

6. Quoted in James Mooney, "The Ghost Dance Religion and the Sioux Outbreak of 1890," *Fourteenth Annual Report of the Bureau of Ethnology*, pt. 2 (1896), 724–5.

7. Ibid.

8. James Doty, *The Journal of Operations of Governor Isaac Ingalls Stevens of Washington Territory in 1855* (Fairfield, Wash.: Ye Galleon Press, 1978), 18.

9. Ibid.

10. Ibid.

11. Ibid., 28.

12. Col. Lawrence Kip, "Indian Council at Walla Walla," facsimile (Seattle: The Shorey Book Store, 1971), 19–20.

13. Ibid., 22.

14. Doty, *Journal of Operations*, 93–4.

15. Ibid., 18–9.

16. Confederated Tribes of the Warm Springs Reservation of Oregon, *The People of Warm Springs* (Warm Springs, Ore.: Confederated Tribes, 1984).

17. Fay G. Cohen, *Treaties on Trial: The Continuing Controversy over Northwest Indian Fishing Rights.* (Seattle: University of Washington Press, 1986), 77–80.

18. Mooney, "Ghost Dance Religion," 721.

"Dr. McKay's Chinook Address May 11 1892": A Commemoration in Chinook Jargon of the First Columbia River Centennial

BY HENRY ZENK

$\mathcal{A}$t first glance, "Dr. McKay's Chinook Address," composed by Dr. William C. McKay for the first Columbia River centennial held on May 11, 1892, offers little of substance. But then, the audience gathered at Astoria for the program of speeches had probably had quite enough of substance by the time Dr. McKay stepped to the platform. From early in the afternoon until well into the evening, these people had been sitting patiently through one long speech after another, as a host of dignitaries provided them with ample opportunity to reflect on the occasion of Captain Robert Gray's entrance into the mouth of the Columbia River on May 11, 1792. Contemporary accounts of the proceedings suggest that Dr. McKay's brief "Chinook address," coming last in the program, pro-vided a pleasing respite after what, for many, must have been a rather long day.

Time evidently has not diminished and has, if anything, enhanced the novelty value of his modest contribution.[1] But the passage of time has also enhanced the value of the speech in ways that could not have been foreseen in Dr. McKay's own time. As a cultural artifact reflecting the composer, his world, and his era, it possesses far more significance now than it ever had as a mere piece of entertainment. Deeper considerations of the language in which the speech was performed, as well as of the performer himself, will reveal much about the new society that took root in the Pacific Northwest as the first permanent European and Euroamerican residents established themselves here. We will be reminded that the early history of the region is not exhausted by the doings of these newcomers, however carefully balanced by all due consideration to the region's indigenous inhabitants. This is also the story of how people from culturally and racially disparate backgrounds met, mingled, and, in quite a few instances, mated.

To begin this excursus into the broader socio-historical implications of Dr. McKay's bit of light entertainment, I draw your attention to the well-documented fact that English, that greatest of international languages, has not always been the principal international language along the Great River of the West. Dr. McKay spoke in Chinook Jargon, a hybrid vernacular that draws its vocabulary from local indigenous languages, especially those once spoken along the lower Columbia River, as well as from French and English. When the indigenous peoples of the Greater Lower Columbia were still a power to be reckoned with, and while such few whites as were in the region were still primarily engaged in the fur trade, Chinook Jargon served traders and Indians as a *lingua franca*, a shared language of the greater multi-lingual region.

Before going further, let's clear up a point of terminology. The title of Dr. McKay's address refers to the language as "Chinook," a usage that has enjoyed wide historical and regional currency. I prefer to be more precise, because the same name also enters history with reference to the Chinook proper language, formerly spoken by the Chinook people, whose ancestral lands are on the north side of the mouth of the Columbia River. Although today we most often hear the word as "sha-nŭk'," the pronunciation "cha-nŭk'" is closer to the original indigenous form of the name. According to our best information, the name was originally given to the Chinook people by their neighbors to the north, the Lower Chehalis people. In the Lower Chehalis language, the name is pronounced *ts'inúk*.[2]

These *ts'inúk* people, along with their cultural and linguistic brethren on the south shore of the mouth of the Columbia River, the *tɬáts'əp*,[3] that is, Clatsop people, were deeply involved in the earliest phase of the Columbia River fur trade (late eighteenth to early nineteenth centuries). Their location, which put them in an ideal position for receiving visits from British and Yankee trading ships, was a crucial factor in that involvement. In 1811, the first permanent trading post on the lower Columbia River, Astoria, was established by the American-owned Pacific Fur Company. Not long afterwards came the War of 1812, one result of which was the transfer of the Astorians' assets, including many of their employees, to the North West Company of Canada. Hence, Astoria became Fort George.

It is in the writings of the Astorians and "Nor'Westers," as employees of the North West Company were known, that we first encounter the ambiguity of reference that has dogged the name "Chinook" ever since. Without a doubt, "Chinook" was originally an English speaker's way of saying the name of the people with whom the early traders carried on much of their business—the *ts'inúk*. But the name rapidly came into use to refer also to those other indigenous groups of the region that most closely resembled the *ts'inúk*—beginning with the *tɬáts'əp* and ascending both sides of the Columbia River (by some early accounts, at least as far up as the Cascades). By extension, it came to mean the closely related languages and dialects spoken by these peoples, the languages linguists now term "Chinookan."[4] But more to the point here, the name came into use also for the intertribal *lingua franca* of the lower Columbia, a language based in large measure on the language of the *ts'inúk* and used extensively during this period by both traders and Indians.

The deeper history of Chinook Jargon has long provoked heated disagreement among scholars. At the nub of the controversy is whether an indigenous *lingua franca* existed on the lower Columbia before the arrival of white traders. Since the issues raised by this question are sufficiently multifarious and complex to warrant an independent treatment, I hope you will forgive me for skirting them here.[5] For our purposes, it suffices to note only that whenever and however the language actually originated, in its developed form it shows a much clearer Indian than European impress. Its sound system and grammar owe more to *ts'inúk* than to any other language. So, it is indeed aptly named Chinook Jargon. Also, as long as I retain the Indian pronunciation for the people originally bearing the name, I am able to avoid the ambiguity of reference first encountered in the writings of the early traders: *ts'inúk* certainly sounds different from "Chinook" (cha-nùk′!).

When early-day white traders and pioneers wrote about learning or speaking "Chinook," it is virtually a sure bet that they were referring to Chinook Jargon, notwithstanding the term's inherent ambiguity in English. The reason is not far to seek. For an English or French speaker, the grammar of a real Chinookan language would prove at least as difficult to master as that of Hungarian or Turkish. On top of that, the phonetic system would be virtually impossible to master without specialized training—unless, of course, one just happened to have grown up with such a language. So you can see why whites almost invariably preferred to learn Chinook Jargon. True, if you want to learn to speak Chinook Jargon like an Indian—what some of the elderly Indian speakers I worked with referred to as "good Jargon," as opposed to "poor Jargon," generally favored by whites—you do have to deal with some of the phonetic difficulty. But the grammar, at least, is much more accessible.

The settlement of the first resident fur traders at the mouth of the Columbia River has a further special relevance to this discussion. Being just a few white men in a sea of Indians, the Astorians and Nor'Westers, naturally enough, strove to be on the best possible terms with their native neighbors. Because they also had something the Indians wanted very much—trade goods (the mercantile orientation of the *ts'inúk* and their neighbors is legendary)—the Indians also had an incentive to make the relationship an amicable one. On the lower Columbia, it happens that the time-honored way of securing the peace and goodwill of other people was to have your daughters marry them. Consequently, a number of the traders married into families of the local chiefs.

Among the first group of these traders to arrive in the Pacific Northwest was Alexander McKay, a Scotsman from Canada, and his part-

Ojibwa teen-aged son, Thomas. Alexander McKay perished in the loss of the Astorians' ship *Tonquin* at Vancouver Island in 1811. Thomas McKay remained in the region and was still quite a young man when he took as his first wife a daughter of the most prominent *ts'inúk* chief of the time, the famous *qanqámli*,[6] known to the whites as Concomly. In about 1824, at Fort George, there was born to this couple a son, christened William Cameron McKay, the self-same Dr. McKay who composed the Chinook Jargon address examined here.

Everyone who knows anything about Chinook Jargon has no doubt heard that it was a "trade language." While that is not an inaccurate characterization, it is not the whole story. It was also a language of family households in the Pacific Northwest's early racially mixed communities. The first such households were established by European and Euroamerican fur company employees who married local Indian women, households like that of the young Dr. McKay.

While we lack documentation of William McKay's early family life, there are some later references to the linguistic characteristics of the region's racially mixed families. Horatio Hale, for example, a pioneer linguist (they were called philologists in those days), visited the Oregon Country in the early 1840s with the United States Exploring Expedition under Charles Wilkes. Concerning the mixed community that had grown up in the Hudson's Bay Company regional base of operations at Fort Vancouver, Hale wrote:

> The place at which the Jargon [Chinook Jargon] is most in use is at Fort Vancouver. At this establishment five languages are spoken by about five hundred persons,—namely, the English, the Canadian French, the Tshinuk [Chinook], the Cree or Knisteneau, and the Hawaiian. . . . Besides these five languages, there are many others,—the Tsihailish [Chehalis], Walawala, Kalapuya, Naskwale [Nisqually], &c., which are daily heard from natives who visit the fort for the purpose of trading. Among all these individuals, there are very few who understand more than two languages, and many who speak only their own. The general communication is, there-

fore, maintained chiefly by means of the Jargon, which may be said
to be the prevailing idiom. There are Canadians and half-breeds
married to Chinook women, who only converse with their wives in
this speech,—and it is the fact, strange as it may seem, that many
young children are growing up to whom this factitious language is
really the mother-tongue, and who speak it with more readiness
and perfection than any other.[7]

Hale's observation gives me an opening to say something about how *I*
learned enough Chinook Jargon to attempt to reconstruct and interpret
the Chinook Jargon of someone whose knowledge of the language very
likely began in childhood.

While my own knowledge does not run so deep, what I do know I
had the privilege of gathering from people for whom Chinook Jargon was a language of family and childhood. The home community of
these people, the Grand Ronde Indian community in northwestern
Oregon, was first established as an Indian reservation in 1856. More recently, it was restored to full federal recognition, following the lately ter-
minated "termination" phase of federal Indian policy. There is actually
a direct historical connection between the families that Hale described
and the Grand Ronde community. For example, the Petite family of
Grand Ronde, a number of whose members I worked with during my
Chinook Jargon research, traces its lineage directly back to the French-
speaking Hudson's Bay Company employee Aimable Petit (*sic*), who
married a Chinookan woman, Susanne Tewatcon, at Fort Vancouver on
March 27, 1837.

Not all Grand Ronde families in which Chinook Jargon was used trace
themselves back to the region's old mixed communities. Among such
families are many with purely Indian genealogies. The point is that Chinook Jargon, what Hale called "this factitious language," penetrated into
many Grand Ronde family households, both Indian and ethnically
mixed. This is the real reason why the language survived long enough for
me to be able to work with fluent speakers until as late as the early 1980s.
At Grand Ronde community gatherings, you may still overhear elders

bantering in Chinook Jargon. I am sorry to have to report, though, that there are perilously few elders who can still do so.[8]

The mingling of races, cultures, and even languages forms an important part of Dr. McKay's own story, and it is also a part of the story of our region. Dr. McKay's personal historical "pedigree," if we may term it that, speaks particularly eloquently here. As we have seen, one of his grandfathers was the most prominent native chief known to the whites. Through the remarriage of his grandmother Margaret Wadine McKay (widow of Alexander McKay) to Dr. John McLoughlin, Dr. McKay also counted none other than the "father" of white Oregon as a step-grandfather.[9]

Dr. McKay's father, deciding that the boy would be an educated man, initially intended to send him away to school in Scotland. It was at the personal urging of the missionary Dr. Marcus Whitman, who firmly believed that the Oregon Country was going American, that he changed his mind and sent young "Billy" instead to the eastern United States. William McKay pursued a course of medical studies and received his license to practice medicine at the age of nineteen. He then returned to the Northwest, arriving at Fort Vancouver in 1843. He subsequently had an active career as the proprietor of a frontier trading post (from which he managed to escape just ahead of hostile Indians), as a government agent in treaty negotiations with many Northwest Indian tribes, as a commanding officer of the Warm Springs Indian Scouts (during the army's campaign against the Paiutes in 1866–1867), and as a government physician attached to Indian agencies (Warm Springs for some years, then the Klamath reservation, and finally the Umatilla reservation). In the 1870 general election, Dr. McKay was denied the franchise because of his Indian heritage. He sued, but the U.S. district court judge ruled that Dr. McKay was either a British citizen or a member of the Indian community and in neither case was legally entitled to vote. He finally did win redress of that indignity, but it took a special act of Congress and the signature of President Grant.

Dr. McKay's historical pedigree was impressive, considering that most of his pioneer contemporaries had arrived in the Pacific Northwest only in the 1840s and 1850s. Many of these "junior" colleagues were in the audience when Dr. McKay addressed the grand celebration convened at Astoria on May 10 and 11, 1892, to commemorate the first Columbia River centennial. In the extensive coverage devoted to the event by the *Morning Oregonian*, Dr. McKay's participation is mentioned at least twice. There was an "experience meeting" of pioneers on May 10, in which "Dr. McKay gave his remarks in Chinook Jargon, interpreting as he went along." But May 11 was the big day of the celebration. Some of the events of that day obviously influenced Dr. McKay as he composed his Chinook Jargon address. In fact, they provide evidence that the address was composed rather shortly before being delivered (it is not impossible that it was written down *after* being delivered).[10]

The festivities on May 11 commenced with a procession of steamships. All the harbor's ships and boats, which included two visiting U.S. Navy cruisers, were decked out in flags and bunting. The barkentine *Chehalis*, fitted out and re-christened for the occasion as Captain Robert Gray's famous ship *Columbia*, led the procession. As the procession returned to Astoria harbor, the visiting cruisers fired salutes, which were greeted by "a general blowing of whistles." The *Oregonian* reporter commented on the general enthusiasm dominating this point of the festivities:

> The bands on various steamers played national airs, and the cheers from hundreds of throats rent the air. The scene was never to be effaced from memory. . . . Tears sprang to many eyes, and a proud consciousness of the national greatness found expression in excited shouts, unexcelled in vigor by the booming of cannon and screaming of whistles.

We have, however, gotten ahead of ourselves. Returning to the initial procession:

> It was about 10 o'clock when Fort Stevenson was breasted, and a salute from its guns acknowledged. The procession then made a

detour east in Baker's Bay, the Columbia casting anchor in the spot where captain Gray is reported to have anchored 100 years ago. . . .

No sooner had anchor been dropped than two canoes were seen pulling out from the northern shore. This feature of the programme proved to be a surprise, cleverly planned and executed by the committee, and kept from the general knowledge of the occupants. They were genuine Chinook canoes, and proved to be a delegation of Chinook, Gray's Harbor, and Shoalwater Bay Indians, imported for the occasion. They carried out their part very neatly, trading salmon with the members of the ship.

Dr. McKay delivered his Chinook Jargon speech as part of the program of orations and addresses occupying the afternoon and early evening of the same day. The *Oregonian* reporter observed, somewhat laconically perhaps, that "a crowded audience listened patiently to addresses from 2:30 until 7 o'clock." Dr. McKay's brief address came last in the program:

> Dr. W. C. McKay, of Pendleton, was then introduced, and made a pleasing address. He spoke briefly and by request in the Chinook language, with which many in the audience were sufficiently familiar to follow him.

There is no published transcript of the speech that I have been able to locate, but there is in Dr. McKay's personal papers (as called to my attention by professor Theodore Stern at the University of Oregon) a short, untranslated Chinook Jargon text. The text is clearly in the doctor's handwriting and bears the title: "Dr. McKay's Chinook Address, May 11, 1892." [11] The text appears on printer's stationery, suggesting that it was intended for publication. It is easy to see, however, why any printer might have thought twice before making the attempt. Dr. McKay's spelling of Chinook Jargon words betrays an intuitively guided attempt to represent, by means of the English alphabet, a typically *Indian* manner of pronunciation. The only trouble is that a number of sounds inherent to such a pronunciation simply do not exist in English.

I now offer the speech for your consideration, with my apologies for burdening it with some technical apparatus. Bear in mind that the language Dr. McKay is attempting to write lacks a standardized orthography, and the attempt definitely requires interpretation. So, on to the apparatus.

The *transcribed text*, which comes at the head of each line-set below, provides my readings of Dr. McKay's scrawling handwriting. Crossed-out words appear so in the original, and raised words correspond to inserted words in the original. Brackets enclose unclear or doubtful readings. Note the unusual punctuation marks and placement of underlined words: these features also characterize samples of Dr. McKay's written English.

The *transliterated text* (second line of each set) reflects my own experience with elderly speakers of the Grand Ronde Community, granting some allowance for small deviations (for example, *fáya* 'fire,' would be *páya* for those speakers, *tílikams* 'people,' would be *tílixam*). I have let the transliterated text stand basically as read before the conference audience, although I have since come to question my initial interpretations of some points. The latter are addressed in footnotes to the text and translation.

The simplified *technical alphabet* used in the transliterated text is meant to reproduce an Indian pronunciation. Sounds shared with English are spelled as in English, with the understanding that *á*, *í*, and *ú* usually have the long values as in father, machine, and June, while *i* and *u* usually have the "short" values in hit and put. The letter *ə* appears for the sound in English but, and the letter *ʔ* for the "catch" in English "uh–oh." For sounds not shared with English, I borrow the following symbols from the Americanist alphabet, which is widely used for writing North American indigenous languages: *ɬ*, a voiceless "l" accompanied by an audible rush of air; *tɬ*, "*ɬ*" said with the tongue initially in position for "t"; *q*, a "k" produced deep in the throat; *x*, a sound like that of *ch* in German

Bach; x̌a "*x*" produced deep in the throat; and *k'*, *p'*, *t'*, *tɬ'*, *ts'*, "exploded" consonants made by suddenly releasing air trapped behind the glottis as one articulates the indicated sound. Stressed words are pronounced more loudly than unstressed ones; like any other language, Chinook Jargon has a characteristic cadence or rhythm. Note that in some words, the stress-bearing syllable may shift in response to this rhythm (examples are the word for 'here', spelled both *yákwa* and *yakwá*, and the name Chinook, spelled both *chinúk* and *chínuk*). To lend further spoken-language authenticity to the text, the reader may also wish to add a degree of stress to the *first* of any two unstressed words preceding a stressed word or compound (for example, **ukuk** *naika ílihi*; **pus** *nəsaika mámuk yútɬit*). The *translations* (third and fourth lines of each set) are my own.

Dr. McKay's Chinook Address May 11 1892

=Nesica olman tilicoms. eleap chaco quapa[12] oco[a]k [I]lihi=

nəsaika úlman tílikams íləp cháku   ukuk ílihi

our senior people first come   this country

Our older people first arrived at this place,[13]

                        poos

Thalsca wawa quapa nesica.   chaco yaqua quapa Astoria-

łaska wáwa kupa nəsáika pus cháku yákwa kupa *Astória*

they say to us for come here to Astoria

they've asked us to come here to Astoria,

    ocock

quapa   Nica ilihi=

kupa ukuk naika ílihi

to that my country

to that which is my own place,

po[o]s nesica m[o]mook yo[ ]tilth quapa nesica tomtom.

pus nəsaika mámuk yútɬił   nəsaika təmtəm

for we make glad   our heart

so that we may make merry.

thlasca
yaqua con[ ]we tilcom   lowlow.
yakwá kánawi   tílkam łaska lú?lu
here   all   people   they   accumulate
Here all the people are gathered.

thlasa chaco yaqua. quapa Chinook thlasca. Mamook sk[ ]kum yoatolth
                                                                         x
        yakwá kupa chinúk łaska   mámuk skúkum yútłił
        here   at   Chinook they   make   strong   glad
Here at Chinook they're having a really fine time.

thalsa. [mook] [thlasa] quapa thlasca House. thlasa Ship.
łaska [múk]   kupa łaska háus   łaska shíp
they   [make?, do?]   at   their house their ship
[They're doing (it) in their homes, their ships—

        [Hiyu] Ship. [quapa] [o]aihat-
        [háyu] shíp [kupa] [úix̌at]
        [many] ship [on]   [road]
        lots of ships—on the road—][14]

conawe [eacta]. thlasa mamook meatwhit thlasa (Sanday ([?])
kánawi [íkta]   łaska mámuk mítxwit łaska [shantéi?]
all   [thing] they   make   stand   they [sing?]
[They've set everything up—they sing.]

        [unintel.]
thlasa   poo hias   moskit=
łaska [mámuk?] p'ú háyash máskit
they   [make?]   shoot big   gun
They fire the cannon.

                                   mamook   yacha
pe ocock fia ship SteamBoat. (thlasa   hoothoot   whistle)=
pi ukuk fáya shíp   łaska mámuk húthut   yax̌ka *whístle*
and that fire ship   they make   "hoot-hoot" its   "whistle"
And that "fire ship" (steamboat)—they sound its whistle.

pe   eact[a] [ocoac]   thlasa mamook Hayash Yo-atolth
                                                        x
pi   íkta   úkuk   łaska mámuk hayásh yútłił

and what   that-one they   make   big   glad

And what it is they make (such) a big time (about):

            100 tacomonoc cool
Ancate   eecht ship yacha chaco quapa ocoac chock=

ánqati   ták'umunaq   kúl íxt   shíp yax̌ka cháku kupa ukuk chúq

long-ago 100   year one ship it   come to   this   water

Long ago, 100 years (ago), a certain ship came to this river,

        yaqua quapa Chinook Ilihi

        yakwá kupa chínuk ílihi

        here   at   Chinook country

        here at Chinook country.

Yacha mash yacha Checimin quapa   [yacha] meatwhiot=

yax̌ka másh yax̌ka   chíkəmin kupá   [yax̌ka] mítxwit

it   throw its   metal   over-there[15] it   stand

It dropped its "metal," over there it stood,

        quapa ocock nica ilihe
                              x
        kupa ukuk naika ílihi

        at   that my   country

        in that which is my own place.

ococ[ ] ship yacha name Columbia=

ukuk   shíp yax̌ka ním   Colúmbia

that   ship its   name Columbia

That ship's name was (the) "Columbia."

pe   alta quaqua ocock nesica highas cho[o]k yacha escem-

pi   álta kákwa   ukuk nəsaika háyash chúq   yax̌ka ískam

and then that-way that   our   big   water it   get

And now that's the way this river of ours got (it),

ocock name Columbia=
ukuk ním   Colúmbia
that   name Columbia
the name "Columbia."

pe   yacha Tayi Captain   yacha name Gray=
pi   yaẋka táyi cáptain   yaẋka ním   Gráy
and its   boss "captain" his   name Gray
And its boss's, the captain's, name was "Gray."

yacha mamook name= tanas sahalie [lowloo] cho[o]k Grays Bay=
yaẋka mámuk ním   tənəs sáẋali   [lúʔlu-] chúq   Gráys Báy
he   make   name   little above [round] water   Grays Bay
He created the name for the bay at bit above [here], "Grays Bay."

conawe sawash thlaska ayack   tigiath makook=
kánawi sawásh łaska áyaq   tq'íẋ   mákuk
all   Indian they   quickly want   trade
All the Indians immediately wanted to trade [with him].

thlasa thlatowa quapa ocock ship q[uapa] thlasa conem
łaska łátuwa   kupa ukuk shíp kupa   łaska kəním
they go   to   that ship in   their canoe
They went to that ship in their canoes.

　　　　[lolo]
thlasa   Ena   Nonamooks. [patabh]
łaska [lúlu] ína   nínamuks   [?]
they   bring beaver otter   [?]
They brought beaver, otter, . . .

Ocock Capt.   yacha nanach holloyoma tilicom ocock
ukuk cáptain yaẋka nánich ẋəlúima   tílikam úkuk
that   captain he   see   different   people that-one
The captain saw that these were a different [strange] people.[16]

(cata thlasca) thlagath thlasca siyahose.

qáta łáska łáq'ał łaska siyáxus

how them flat   their eye/forehead

[And] how it was with them: their foreheads were flat,[17]

thlasca latote quaqua pos   [[Y]oatchot]- Hayash thlasca labosh.

łaska latét kákwa pus[18] [yútsqat]   hayásh łaska lapúsh

their head like as [short]   big   their mouth

their heads looked [short], their mouths were big,

thlasca siya[hos] th=

łaska siyáxus [łk'úp?]

their forehead [squeezed]

their foreheads were [pressed].[19]

= quapa alta yacha mamook thlasca latote canawe thlagath=

kupá álta yaẍka mámuk łaska latét kánawi łáq'ał

there then it   made   their head all   flat

There then it [?] caused their heads to be all flat.[20]

pe   yacha chlose tomtom quapa ocock tilicoms=

pi   yaẍka łúsh tə́mtəm kupa ukuk tílikams

and he   good heart to   those people

And he was very well disposed to those people.

mowatch

thlasa mamook chaco. Salmon   [eathlwit]

łaska mámuk cháku sámən máwich [ítsẍwət]

they make   come salmon deer [black-bear]

They brought salmon, deer, bear,

pi   conawi eacta chlose pose macemuck-

pi   kánawi íkta łúsh pus mə́k(ə)mək

and all   thing good for eat

and all things good to eat.

Pe   alta [thlasa] macook thlasa. <u>Eena</u>   <u>nonomooks-</u>
pi   álta [łaska] mákuk łaska ína   nínamuks
and then [they] trade   their beaver otter
And then they traded their beaver and otter.

[hiyoyo]   thlasca <u>macook</u> quapa <u>yacha</u>=
[háyu-hayu?] łaska   mákuk kupa yáx̌ka
[lots-lots?]   they   trade   with   him
They traded [many things?] with him [Capt. Gray].

NOTES

1. This observation reflects the gratifying response I received upon reading my appended transliteration of Dr. McKay's text to the audience.

2. The words *ts'inúk* and *tłáts'əp* appear in the same simplified technical orthography used to transliterate Dr. McKay's speech (note that in the appended transcript, the transliterated text appears directly below Dr. McKay's text). The values of the symbols used are explained in the notes prefacing the speech.

3. See note 2.

4. The linguistic distribution and ethnography of the lower Columbia Chinookans are sketched by Michael Silverstein, "Chinookans of the Lower Columbia," *Handbook of North American Indians*, vol. 7 (Washington, D.C.: Smithsonian Institution, 1990), 533–46.

5. Recent contributions to the discussion are (arguing for pre-contact origin) Dell Hymes, "Commentary," *Theoretical Orientations in Creole Studies*, ed. Albert Valdman and Arnold Highfield (New York, 1980), 389–423; Sarah Thomason, "Chinook Jargon in Areal and Historical Context," *Language* 59:4 (1983): 820–70; and (arguing for post-contact origin) William Samarin, "Chinook Jargon and Pidgin Historiography," *Canadian Journal of Anthropology* 5:1 (1986): 23–34.

6. Like the other indigenous-language forms cited, this one uses the orthography explained for the appended Jargon text. (We have the daughter's name as Timmee, but since the source is not a linguist's transcription, the accuracy of the *ts'inúk* is in doubt.)

7. Horatio Hale, "Ethnography and Philology," *U.S. Exploring Expedition During the Years 1838, 1839, 1840, 1841, 1842*, vol. 6 (Philadelphia, 1846), 644.

8. I would like to acknowledge the following past and present Grand Ronde

elders who taught me Chinook Jargon: Mr. Wilson Bobb, Sr., Mr. Dellmore Croy, Mrs. Ila Dowd, Mrs. Esther LaBonte, Mrs. Ethel Logan, Mrs. Martha Mercier, Mr. and Mrs. John and Eula Petite, and Mrs. Clara Riggs.

9. For a well-researched sketch of Dr. McKay's life, see Keith Clark and Donna Clark, "William McKay's Journal, 1866–67: Indian Scouts," *Oregon Historical Quarterly* 79 (Summer 1978): 121–71; (Fall 1978): 269–333. See also "Dr. W. C. McKay," *East Oregonian* (Pendleton), January 2, 1889.

10. My account of the festivities draws on the *Morning Oregonian* reports of May 11 and 12, 1892.

11. Papers of Dr. William C. McKay, Oregon Collection MF 27, University of Oregon Library, Eugene.

12. Dr. McKay has first written in, then crossed out the universal preposition *quapa*. Grand Ronde speakers often omit the preposition after the verbs *cháku*, 'come,' and *ɬát(u)wa*, 'go'. Note also that Dr. McKay's spelling of this frequently used word is consistent throughout the text, suggesting a pronunciation deviating from my regionally more familiar transliteration form (*kupa*). A number of other words suggest similar points of difference: *quaqua*, 'like, in that manner' (my *kákwa*); *thlasa*, third person plural pronoun (for *ɬasa*, variant of regional *ɬaska*?; Dr. McKay also spells the word *thlasca*, etc.); and *yacha*, third person singular pronoun (for *yaxa*, variant of regional *yaxka*?).

13. When I first looked at the speech, I puzzled over this line. *úlman tílikams* (I would say *tílixam*) evidently refers to senior people who had already arrived (*íləp cháku*), but who would that be? Some of the speaker's relatives or friends? It was only after reading newspaper accounts of the event that it occurred to me that this was probably the doctor's way of referring to the assembled pioneers. There is no word specifically meaning 'pioneer' in Jargon. When one lacks a word for something in this language, one generally compounds existing words to suggest the basic idea. This is a nice illustration of the linguistic creativity that is integral to successful communication in Jargon.

14. The brackets enclosing my translations of this and the next set signify that their interpretation remains uncertain.

15. For Grand Ronde speakers, the form *kupa* (or *kapa*) may function either as a preposition (in which case it is ordinarily unstressed) or as a demonstrative adverb meaning '(over)-there' (stressed: *kupá, kapá*). While Dr. McKay's text provides no basis for drawing conclusions about stress, the placement of his form *quapa* here suggested to me that he shared the functional distinction. On subsequent reflection, however, it appears likely that *quapa* is functioning here as a subordinating conjunction (a linking word introducing a subordinate

clause), as attested in some varieties of Jargon, though not in that of Grand Ronde speakers. The sentence, retransliterated and retranslated to reflect the latter interpretation, would read: *yax̌ka másh yax̌ka chíkəmin kupa yax̌ka mítxwit*, or 'It dropped its "metal" so that it stood fast. . . .'

16. Literally, 'that captain sees different people these (are)'—good Jargon syntax.

17. It is tempting to interpret *łáq'ał* as a transitive verb ('to flatten') in order to make the parenthesized phrase "(cata <u>thlasca</u>)" fall somewhat more naturally into place: 'That captain saw that these were a different people, (how they) flattened their foreheads.' I do not adopt the latter reading, however, because in the Chinook Jargon with which I am familiar, a modifying element (*mamuk* in Dr. McKay's jargon, *munk* in that of Grand Ronde speakers) would be required to turn *łáq'ał*, attested with the adjectival meaning 'flat,' into a corresponding transitive verb. On the other hand, speakers' perceptions as to the inherent adjectival or active meanings of particular words may vary somewhat.

18. *kákwa pus*, 'looks like [it]' (usually reduced in form to *kákupus*) was a common idiom at Grand Ronde.

19. I originally read this line as "their (*siyáxus:*) eyes were [(*tɬ'íp:*) sunken in]." Later, I arrived at the more plausible reading appearing here: 'their (*siyáxus:*) foreheads were [(*łk'úp* 'squeezed':) pressed].'

20. Again, I read *kapá*, used by Grand Ronde speakers as a demonstrative adverb, for Dr. McKay's *quapa*. Reinterpreted and retranslated (see note 15), the sentence (with the line preceding) would read: '. . . their foreheads were [pressed?], so that it caused their heads then to be all flat.'

Riverplaces as Sacred Geography:
The Pictographs and Petroglyphs
of the Mid-Columbia River

BY WILLIAM D. LAYMAN

The Columbia River evokes thoughts and feelings as expansive and large as the river itself, shaped not only by an awareness of how the river functions in our lives but, as importantly, through highly personal responses to its many turnings and moods. For those of us living within its watershed, the Columbia is always near. We take its waters into our bodies and minds. Even from the comfort of our living rooms we stay alert to the ways of this river, its presence repeatedly sounded through headlines announcing radioactive groundwater movement at Hanford, struggling salmon runs on the verge of extinction, or ever escalating Bonneville Power Administration electric rates. In the back of our minds we hold the difficult knowledge that this highly regulated and complex water system is attempting to fill too many functions for too many species, its once wild waters held back again and again by the vast dams that power our days and light our nights.

For native people whose early life centered along the Columbia's shorelines, mention of the river they know as *niawana* (Sahaptin) and *netqua* (Salishan) brings feelings of profound grief over what has been lost. For them, the river covers homelands—villages of their families, fisheries of their people, and a way of life that has been thousands of years in the making. Among the elders are those who remember the un- tamed river, its rapids surging over familiar landscapes that hold the myths and stories of their people. They know the specific places where the tule grew and where sturgeon were once caught. They know, too, the rock formations on whose submerged surfaces depictions of animals, humans, and supernatural beings were once seen. These remembered places embody their people's spiritual traditions and provide a link, a continuity of experience.

With the passing years, the number of native people who remember the unaltered Columbia grows fewer. Without the elders to describe the excitement of the river's free-flowing nature, the young people are in- creasingly challenged to see rocks and rapids where none remain. Yet, the need to feel kinship with these riverplaces is strong, rising from deep within a culture and a history shaped by the river. By listening to stories passed down through oral traditions, participating in tribal ritual and practices, and viewing historical photographs, succeeding generations can come to know they are never far from the river of their ancestors, never far from those storied rocks beneath the water (see fig. 1).

Much of the basalt rock found along the Columbia has smooth sur- faces, which lends itself well to both painting images (pictographs) and scratching or pecking out designs (petroglyphs). Some of images, such as *Tsagiglalal* at Horsethief Lake State Park, have gained a great measure of notoriety, while others remain unknown except to a few scholars and native people. Most of the pictographs and petroglyphs have long been flooded by the dams on the river. This is certainly true of over thirty sites located along the mid-Columbia between Priest Rapids and Rock Island. The documentation efforts undertaken long ago have been stored and forgotten in museum and university archives, so the sites are not well known in spite of being one of the richer concentrations of pic- tographs and petroglyphs in the Pacific Northwest. Three of the major sites—Whale Island at Priest Rapids, Rock Island Rapids, and Cabinet Rapids—were situated on islands between channels of fast water (see fig. 2). Others, including those near the town of Vantage, as well as the

Fig. 1 Puck Hyat Toot (Frank Buck) looking upriver toward Sentinel Gap prior to the building of Priest Rapids Dam. (Grant County PUD photograph)

Fig. 2 Petroglyphs at Rock Island depicting two American bighorn sheep. Prized by Plateau Native American people for fur and food, bighorn sheep are more prevalent in rock art panels than any other animal throughout the western United States. (Harold Simmer photograph, c. 1930, North Central Washington [NCW] Museum, Wanatchee, WA)

Sentinel Bluff, Whiskey Dick, and Spanish Castle sites, were positioned on large columns of volcanic basalt rising prominently from the shoreline. The Wenatchee, Columbia, Kittitas, and Wanapum peoples identify these sites as homelands.

Throughout the English-speaking world, the term "rock art" is currently used to describe these images. Yet, native people of the Columbia Plateau and elsewhere find this term difficult to fathom. Adeline Fredin, tribal historian of the Colville Confederated Tribes, asserts that native people never have considered pictographs or petroglyphs as *art*, a European word imposed on Indian people. She regards the figures as part of a historical record, a written history that tells the story of her people.

Pictographs and petroglyphs are generally divided by archaeologists into three broad categories, all of which are represented in central Washington. Figures closely resembling known animals such as sheep or deer are referred to as *naturalistic*. Those figures suggesting animals or supernatural beings but bearing little direct likeness to them are known as *stylized*. A third category, *abstract*, consists of lines, dots, and circles arranged in distinct patterns. These rock graphics exhibit regional stylistic variations. In the mid-Columbia region, four distinct styles have been identified. Most of the pictographs and petroglyphs found above The Dalles fit within the *Columbia Plateau* style. Its primary characteristics include human figures (often with rays extending from their heads), naturalistic depictions of animals, and abstract designs based on circular or curvilinear motifs (see fig. 3). A few petroglyphs by Priest Rapids can be placed within the highly stylized *Long Narrows* style of the lower Columbia. At sites near Vantage, figures had vivid red and white marks in a circular patterns known as the *Yakima Polychrome* style. At Rock Island Rapids, a boulder with cupules and deep grooves marks a fourth style, *pit and groove*, more commonly found in California and the Great Basin.

Many panels of rock art found in central Washington contain hunting scenes (see fig. 4). For indigenous cultures, hunting was a spiritual endeavor, the undertaking framed in courtesies, prayer, and rules. The frequency of hunting imagery in the rock art points to a possibility that

Fig. 3 Rock Island petroglyph depicting two hunters with bows, animals of the hunt, and shield design. The panel measures approximately seven feet across. (Drawing by Harold Cundy, c. 1930, NCW Museum)

Fig. 4 Rock Island petroglyph of an archer ready to shoot an arrow at a mountain sheep whose horn makes contact with a circular figure. (Harold Simmer photograph, c. 1930, NCW Museum)

the creation of the petroglyphs themselves might have played an important role in the hunt.

While there are rare instances of myths handed down by Columbia Plateau native tribes referring to a story of a figure or a site, the only reliable sources of interpretation of Columbia Plateau pictographs and petroglyphs were the people who were actively engaged in this tradition. Some of these native people were interviewed in the early part of the century. When ethnologist James Teit spoke directly with several of the men who painted rocks in the upper Columbia region, he learned that the images were produced by both adolescents and adults participating in a supernatural experience, perhaps a vision following a quest or a visitation by a spirit figure in a special dream. Amateur archaeologist Harold Cundy was told by several north-central Washington natives that rock paintings were done in conjunction with a person finding his special power (*shoomesh*).

Many of these early inquiries identified the experience of painting and carving images on rocks as highly personal, and meanings were not meant to be shared with others throughout that individual's lifetime. Modern leaders echo that sentiment. Many speak forcefully that the interpretations are not to be trivialized in any way. They caution others against committing the cultural violation of delving too deeply into matters that are not meant to be pursued. The pictographs and petroglyphs are living things to many of these people, imbued with powerful personal and spiritual meanings (see fig. 5). Reproduction, interpretation, or use without consulting the tribes also constitutes a violation.

Traveling through the Columbia's impressive canyons, one clearly sees that the people who painted and engraved these rocks were responding to long-standing relationships with the places around them. Each site possessed unique features and histories that evoked powerful responses. It is not hard to imagine a person experiencing moments of intense feelings at one of these places and having profound visions after a time of praying, fasting, and staring into the moving water. Marking such a time and place by leaving an image on a rock is in keeping with time-honored traditions practiced by peoples throughout the world. The

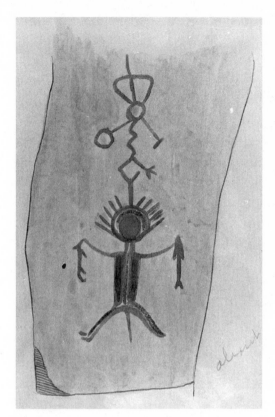

Fig. 5 Pictograph of a human-like figure at Picture Rocks Bay above Vantage. The individual holds an animal and possibly a fish in its hands. Eleven rays emanate from the head. The middle line links the figure to a more abstract second figure with head, arms, and legs. (Drawing by Harold Cundy, c. 1930, NCW Museum)

presence of these images makes a statement to all that here is a place of power where visions were sought and received.

Each generation of river-dwelling people was keenly aware of the ancestors who had preceded them. The first rock art in the region appeared before Mount Mazama erupted some 6,700 years ago. Other petroglyphs and pictographs are thought to be several thousand years old, based on associations from dated portable objects and other stylistic considerations. Much mid-Columbia rock art is clearly of a later vintage. We know, for example, that people used bows and arrows less than 2,500 years ago. Pictographs or petroglyphs showing horses suggest they were made some time after 1730. Some images of buffalo, like one found six miles below Rock Island Rapids, may have been done after the Plateau

Indians made the long and dangerous ride on horses across the Rocky Mountains in pursuit of bison. Billie Curlew of the Columbia Sinkiuse knew an Indian who created a rock art panel near Grand Coulee and who stated that the images found there were pictures of cattle brands made sometime in the early pioneer period.

Other relative dating methods exist. For example, certain photographs of mid-Columbia pictographs and petroglyphs show that the natural finish of a rock (patina), had re-formed over the petroglyphs, indicating they were made long ago (see fig. 6). In recent years, promising scientific methods of dating pictographs and petroglyphs have emerged, although none of these have been tested on inundated sites. To native people, it is enough to know that these mid-Columbia images were created by the Ancients.

In whatever time they were done, the images let us know about a people who valued traditions of place. Root- and berry-gathering areas, hunting grounds, stone quarries, and rock art sites were all used to enhance a particular aspect of cultural life. To this day, descendants of these cultures continue these practices that connect them to their histories of place.

As one of the few tribes that continue to live along the banks of the river, the Wanapum people maintain a profound regard for their flooded homelands. Within their longhouse by Priest Rapids Dam is a photograph showing the tule mat lodges at P'na, their former village (see fig. 7). Another photograph shows an island at the foot of Priest Rapids that was especially important to the Wanapum people. Called Chalwash Chilni, it was where the first beings, One Legged Abalone Man and Sun Man, lived. All life emerged from the island; every bird and animal, every root, plant, tree, and berry was released there from the darkness. From this place came the teachings that formed the distinctive character of the Wanapum culture and religion. Listening to the elders, it is apparent that feelings about the island and the rocks run deep. "In my younger days, we walked on the island with respect," says Wanapum elder Bobby Tomanawash. "We didn't sit or climb on the rocks . . . that's how sacred it was to us."

Fig. 6 Petroglyph from Rock Island Rapids showing a hunter and elk, with a horse and rider to its right. The images have been pecked through the patina of the dense basalt rock found on the island. (Harold Simmer photograph, c. 1930, NCW Museum)

Fig. 7 Village of P'na at Priest Rapids in about 1938. Shown is a flagpole and three tule mat lodges used by the Wanapum people. The village was moved prior to the flooding of Priest Rapids. (Grace Christianson Gardner photograph, NCW Museum)

When Grant County PUD decided to build Priest Rapids Dam, the planners were aware that the new dam would flood both island and village as well as many important places upriver. Therefore, care was taken to respect the island and its rock art. Puck Hyat Toot, an elder of the Wanapums, and other village people were consulted, and a decision was reached to document the rock art before the dam was built. In July 1956, a Grant County PUD staff member took photographs of the petroglyphs. Shortly thereafter, with the start of the University of Washington salvage archaeological program, project leader Dr. Robert Greengo asked graduate student Arlie Ostling to make a complete record of the island's extensive rock art (see fig. 8). Traveling daily to the island by boat during the summer of 1957, she photographed, mapped, and made direct impressions of 137 petroglyphs found on the island. Most of the rock art was clustered on the lower end of this barren island. One unusually large boulder with a stylized face resembling a sea mammal stood out clearly among the rocks. Another boulder depicted bear tracks, an element found more commonly in Idaho. Also unique to the region's rock art were sixteen separate boulders cut with serrated edges. One of the island's most remarkable petroglyphs was covered by intricate patterns of deep grooves. In 1950, when John Campbell surveyed mid-Columbia archaeological sites, he thought the rock's markings suggested a sturgeon's skeleton (see fig. 9). When Arlie Ostling saw it in 1957, she thought it looked more like a reclining sheep. In keeping with Columbia Plateau stylistic traditions, many rocks on the island showed circular and curved patterns, often accompanied by rays. Knowing they would soon be under water, Puck Hyat Toot selected a number of the petroglyphs for removal. Some of them were later placed near a picnic area at the base of Priest Rapids Dam.

While the petroglyphs at Priest Rapids lost their context due to flooding, the rock art at Sentinel Bluff fared even worse because of blasting. Located 1.2 miles south of Crab Creek on the east bank of the Columbia, this site succumbed to several successions of road building, each of which destroyed significant portions of the site. Harlan Smith, the first archaeologist to visit the region in 1903, photographed two areas

Fig. 8 Petroglyph found on Chalwash Chilni (Whale Island) at Priest Rapids. Images of arcs with rays are found throughout the Plateau culture area. (Arlie Ostling photograph , NCW Museum)

Fig. 9 Highly unusual stylized boulder with deep grooves covering the entire rock on Whale Island at Priest Rapids. The lines along the ridge of the rock suggest vertebrae of some animal. Wanapum people regarded the island as sacred and took care never to step or sit on the rocks. (Arlie Ostling photograph, NCW Museum)

containing petroglyphs, one of which was destroyed by road construction shortly after his visit. In 1930, Wenatchee photographer Harold Simmer photographed one of the site's most remarkable petroglyphs before it, too, was blasted to make way for a bigger road (see fig. 10). The primary image is an armless human with four toes on each foot and thirteen rays surrounding its head. Positioned down each side of its body are two columns of ten dots. Figures surrounding the image show another human, sheep, faces, rayed arcs, and a number of incised lines that appear to be randomly distributed. According to evidence of repatination, the figures are older than the designs superimposed on them. Some of the marks resemble bird tracks. Archaeologists, however, have suggested that the incisions may be evidence that the rock was used for sharpening stone tools. Thomas Cain wrote about the Sentinel Bluff site in his 1950 *Petroglyphs of Central Washington*, and Del Nordquist added a far more comprehensive description in 1954, completing all that is known of the site. What road building did not destroy, the backwaters of Priest Rapids Dam did. As is the case with other submerged sites along the Columbia, a full understanding of the Sentinel Gap petroglyphs only emerges by piecing together the work of many.

At Vantage, Washington, Interstate 90 descends and crosses one of the river's most dramatic canyons. A short distance from the highway is Ginkgo Petrified Forest State Park, where visitors can view petroglyphs assembled from several inundated sites once found about a mile upriver. Harold Cundy, a flour salesman and amateur archaeologist, made frequent visits to the Vantage sites beginning in 1930 and accurately recorded the rock art there. Many years later, in 1957, the Vantage sites were professionally documented as part of Grant County PUD's salvage archaeological work. Yet, even with the formal site documentation by graduate student Susan Barrow and photographer Al Deane, the locations of the sites remained in question for many years after the reservoir was flooded. Cundy, Cain, and Barrow had each given different and conflicting information. For example, several key photographs in Barrow's work turned out to be mislabeled. In recent years, researchers have positively identified the submerged sites by taking copies of the University

Fig. 10 Petroglyph at Sentinel Gap. The central figure of the main panel has feet with digits, no arms, and a head encircled by an arch with rays. Rows of dots line either side. The petroglyph was partially destroyed by road construction in the early 1930s. In 1957, the site was inundated by the backwaters of Priest Rapids Dam. (Harold Simmer photograph, NCW Museum)

of Washington survey photographs to the river and lining up their backgrounds with the present water level.

The first of the Vantage sites shows several animals, a man holding a bow and another man with rays emanating from his head (see fig. 11). Susan Barrow probably intended to draw a sketch of the site, but it was not included in her notebook. Fortunately, Cundy's pen-and-ink drawing shows how the images were placed in relation to one another (see fig. 12). Located a short distance upriver, the second Vantage site is composed of approximately fourteen figures, including an interesting pictograph of two humans with hands touching. Called paired anthropomorphs by archaeologists, these twin figures are somewhat rare in North American rock art. The mid-Columbia region has sixteen examples of this type of figure located at seven different sites. While the meaning of these petroglyphs and pictographs remains unclear, twins in numerous Native American and other world mythologies often have supernatural powers.

Several hundred yards upriver, a large columnar basalt formation is the backdrop for the third Vantage site. Reachable only by canoe or when the water is low, it contains more than a hundred pictographs and petroglyphs. The 1957 University of Washington study made full-scale tracings of the figures, assigning each a number. A schematic of the basalt formation showed where the figures were situated on the panel, and the tracings were color coded to differentiate pictographs from petroglyphs. They were then transferred onto 50-foot rolls of clear film. Getting a good sense of the entire site remained problematic until 1991, when reductions of the images were superimposed directly onto the schematic. Knowing where each of the images had been on the river and how the original panel may have looked adds greatly to our understanding.

The panel contains many examples of the elements characteristic of the Columbia Plateau style: human figures, circles with rays, and naturalistic animals. Several of the figures depict hunting. Three twin figures are present, one with a third smaller figure centered between them. Photographs, as well as Cundy's drawing, suggest that the third figure was added by a different artist. Next was a highly unusual human figure with

Fig. 11 The first of four sites above Vantage. Rays emanate from the head of a figure close to ground level. (1957 photograph by Al Deane from University of Washington archaeological work with Grant County PUD; photograph in possession of Grant County PUD)

Fig. 12 Amateur archaeologist Harold J. Cundy at Picture Rocks Bay. Cundy documented over fifty sites throughout north-central Washington between 1928 and 1937. Cundy's skill as an artist and his passion for recording sites place his work among the finest examples of early rock art documentation in the United States. (NCW Museum photograph)

four rays emanating from its head. It appears to be holding objects in both hands. A line crossing below its jaw is connected to two circles, with a similar design beneath the figure. Cundy noted that he had not seen any other figure quite like it on the river.

A mile farther upriver was Picture Rocks Bay, the best known of the Vantage sites. The approach to the site was hazardous, involving walking along a narrow bench high above the water line and then taking a steep descent down a talus slope to the small bay. A series of hexagonal basalt boulders marked the location of the site on the downriver side of the bay. Rising sharply from the shoreline, layers of towering basalt formations added to the site's impressive character. Researcher Susan Barrow documented well over 300 designs at the site and believed that Picture Rocks Bay contained the best examples of pictographs and petroglyphs found along the river.

Harold Cundy compiled a folder of over twenty careful pen-and-ink drawings from the site's figures. The columns are filled with deer, sheep, humans, and rayed arc designs. Petroglyphs prevail, but there are notable pictographs as well. In one instance, two pictographs, one a twin figure and the other a circle executed in the Yakima Polychrome style, are superimposed on one another to make a striking statement. As with other mid-Columbia sites, most figures at Picture Rocks Bay seem to bear no relation to others. Some, particularly deer and sheep figures, appear in clusters and groupings, One panel has a small abstract design at its base, which follows the contour of the rock. The design emphasizes the six leaping deer and sheep figures poised above (see fig. 13). Another panel shows well-defined relationships among several figures. Below are three concentric circles surrounded by twenty-one rays; above is the image of a deer and above it another arc with twenty-one rays. A large anthropomorph is depicted with a spirit figure rising from the middle ray of its head. Several photographs of the site show evidence of vandals. In one, the initials SS, as well as a lightly scratched tipi seem out of place, a reminder of the extremely fragile and vulnerable nature of rock art sites.

Given the extraordinary nature of the Vantage sites, it is little wonder they attracted public attention. For a time, Tom Stockdale of Vantage

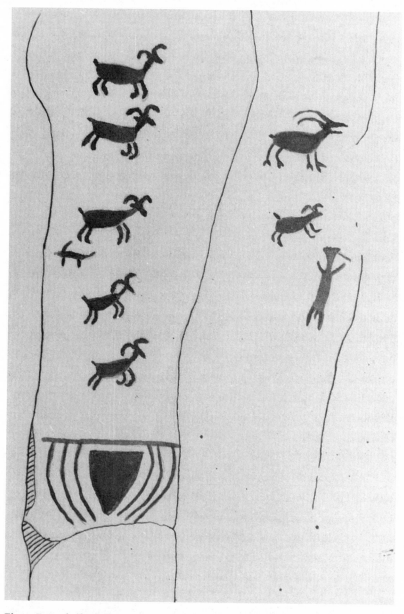

Fig. 13 Petroglyph of Picture Rocks Bay depicting mountain sheep. The abstract design below uses the natural contour of the columnar basalt, giving the panel a visual base that enhances the lower figure's leaping movement. (Harold Cundy drawing of Vantage petroglyph, 1931)

offered motorboat excursions to the picture rocks upriver, but sightseeing came to a stop when the plan to build Wanapum Dam was announced (see fig. 14). Stockdale gathered support from the Columbia Basin Rock Hounds Club and lobbied the state to allocate $20,000 to move many of the petroglyphs to the new visitors center at Ginkgo State Park. By viewing the display, park visitors gain a measure of insight into the submerged legacy of the river. Local native people, however, regard the removal of the figures from the sites with mixed feeling.

Another six miles upriver, a rock formation marks a site covered by 45 feet of water. Thomas Cain located the site in Whiskey Dick Canyon, but the rock art panels were several miles upriver from that canyon. As at Vantage, people here chose the smooth surfaces of columnar basalt on which to paint and carve their images and visions. Among the elements were three paired anthropomorphs. Extending from the heads of one set of the twin figures are five lines giving the appearance of hands. With coastal tribes twins were known to be associated with salmon and had great influence over the annual runs, thus raising the tantalizing possibility that the figures found along the mid-Columbia might themselves be linked to salmon. Near the twins are other designs characteristic of the central Washington area, including a remarkable stylized human figure. Knowing that information on the site would soon be lost, Arlie Ostling recorded the site and its figures, making it possible for future generations to know and feel its presence.

Farther upriver, the Spanish Castle site possessed a number of finely executed petroglyphs, but the rock art here was never fully documented. Only a few photographs, some drawings by Cundy, and Cain's brief description tell of five snake figures we will never see. There is even less information about the rock art of Cabinet Rapids, with only Cundy's drawings to show what was once there. Cundy also made drawings of the Douglas Creek site just across the river on the north bank of Cabinet Rapids. Fortunately, Brian and Susan Holmes, who worked under Dr. Greengo, thoroughly documented this small island in 1963.

Five miles upriver from Cabinet Rapids was a large island surrounded by a cluster of smaller ones. The islands were situated in the middle of

Fig. 14 Postcard image of a tour group visiting Picture Rocks Bay above Vantage. The site's massive hexagonal basalt formations provided many opportunities for placing pecked and painted images on its rock surfaces. The present level of Wanapum Reservoir is approximately 40 feet above the water level shown in the photograph. (NCW Museum)

particularly strong rapids and offered excellent places to fish. To Wenatchi and Columbia natives, the fishery and the habitation site just up-river were known as Kahwah-chin, or "living by the banks." Only a very small part of the island remains behind the Rock Island Dam, and it is hard to imagine the pristine place that fur trader and explorer David Thompson described when he visited here in 1811. In the early 1920s, it was not uncommon for families to take the bumpy road south from Wenatchee and spend their day gathering arrowheads along the riverbanks. Few now remember the original island, and fewer yet have crossed the river to walk on it (see fig. 15).

When construction plans for the dam were announced by Puget Sound Power & Light in 1929, the Columbia River Archaeological Society, formed in 1921, decided to document and salvage the island's rock

Fig. 15 At Rock Island Rapids, the river dropped ten and one-half feet as it cut around both sides of the nearly mile-long island. Various reefs, rocks, and sharply projecting points obstructed the river channels, making passage hazardous as well as providing important habitat for migrating salmon. (Joseph Monosmith photograph, private collection)

Fig. 16 Petroglyph panel at Rock Island Rapids shows an elk figure at upper right. Elsewhere, two archers draw their bows toward animals they are hunting. (Harold Simmer photograph, c. 1930, NCW Museum)

art. They entered into negotiations with the power company and reached an agreement that Harold Simmer would photograph the island's rock art at the company's expense. With his lens, Simmer recorded an enormous variety of beings, including elk, deer, sheep, goats, birds, bear, coyote, a small mammal, and a crawfish. Many humans and supernaturals also were found among the images carved and pecked into the rocks (see fig. 16). All together, the number of elements on the island easily exceeded five hundred, making it one of the largest rock art sites in the Pacific Northwest.

Harold Cundy, a member of the Columbia River Archaeological Society, completed thirty-one pen-and-ink drawings, some of them not recorded in the Simmer collection, including one that depicts an entire herd of elk (see fig. 17). Another set of photographs, taken by Wenatchee physician Thomas Grosvenor, shows additional images not documented by others. Puget Sound Power & Light also agreed to help the society

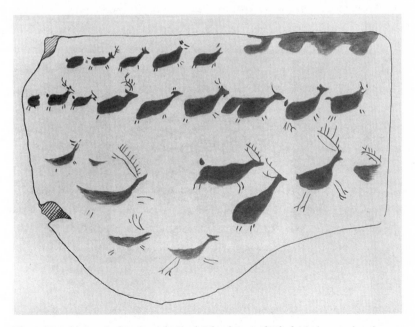

Fig. 17 Harold Cundy drawing of a Rock Island petroglyph depicting a migrating herd of elk. (NCW Museum)

remove thirty-one of the petroglyphs. After various plans were considered, including the base of a bandstand and the Carnagie library building foundation, the petroglyphs were set in gravel behind a chain link fence at the base of the Great Northern locomotive in Wenatchee. For their protection, they were later moved to the historical gallery at Rocky Reach Dam. Additional petroglyphs were moved to the North Central Washington Museum, which dedicated its exhibit to Native Americans who had lived and fished in this area of the Columbia River.

Most photographs of the petroglyphs are close-up views, making it impossible to know where the images were found on the island itself. A precious few photographs offer enough information to reveal that much of the rock art was clustered in an area above a prominent landmark called Hawksbills Point. Although the dam prevents us from visiting the island first hand, these photographs help open the possibilities to our imaginations (see fig. 18).

The pictographs and petroglyphs left by descendants and ancestors of the Wenatchi, Columbia, Kittitas, Wanapum, and Yakama people are primary to the story of the Columbia River between Priest Rapids and Rock Island. The images of birds, four-leggeds, and even coyote share in that story and remind us of a time when animals were regarded as great beings. To the native people, if a person prayed, fasted, and sought the animals' counsel, they would share their special wisdom through a song or a vision filled with power. Such clarifying, life-transforming moments were intimately connected to the islands and shores of this section of the Columbia.

The photographs, drawings, rubbings, and existing rock art serve as present-day connections to these special riverplaces. Before the dams raised the water levels of the river, individuals such as Harold Cundy and Arlie Ostling found a special calling to record the past. The work at Priest Rapids and other sites has been particularly important to present-day Native Americans who want their children to know the sacred landscapes of the past. In the summer of 1991, the young Wanapum children living at the village by Priest Rapids gathered to view for the first time

Fig. 18 Photograph taken from upper end of Rock Island Rapids looking across the river toward the east bank of the Columbia. While many photographs were taken of the island's rock art, this view provides the only solid evidence indicating where the petroglyphs could once be found on the island. (Nitschke photograph, Russell Congdon collection)

the rubbings made from the island's petroglyphs. Rex Buck, grandson of Puck Hyat Toot, told the children of the rubbings' importance and shared that by touching the cloth that touched the rocks they might come to know their sacred island. It was a message in keeping with their religious traditions. The first recorded Wanapum spiritual leader, Shuawpsa, told his people the Creator's wish: "Sing and dance so that I may know you are remembering." The rock art of the mid-Columbia stands as a bridge upon which to build that memory. In so doing, children of Native Americans throughout the region might come to find their place in the story of this great river.

On the Columbia:
The Ruling Presence of This Place

BY JAMES P. RONDA

The author of the line that gives title to this essay is Wendell Berry. On first hearing, his Appalachian mountain voice may seem an odd guide for any voyage on the Columbia. His country is the Cumberland and the Blue Ridge; his rivers the Kentucky, the Licking, and the Holston. But like many other American writers, Wendell Berry has grasped something fundamental about land, rivers, and the lives of all creatures. The whole of what he writes is this: "The river is the ruling presence of this place. The mind, no matter how free of it, is always tempted and tugged at by the nearness of the water and the clear space over it, ever widening and deepening into the continent." Definition and expression—that is what rivers have given to the cultures of the continent. Rivers have defined the spaces, marked the boundaries. They are nature's survey. In them we read the expressions, the aspirations, the mad dreams and schemes of men and women drawn to the river. Gretel Ehrlich writes, "To trace the history of a river is to trace the history of the soul." The Columbia has, in one way or another, been the "ruling presence" of this country. To comprehend its many histories, its many images, is to catch something of the story of the soul. We have invented the Columbia over and over again, each time investing it with an identity that says more about us than this ribbon of twisting water. Reading it, we read ourselves until at last the river becomes, as T. S. Eliot said it would, a piece of the inside of us.

In the beginning it was Nch'i-Wána, the big river. As Gene Hunn eloquently writes in his book of the same name, the river forms "the spine" of the land, the "core of the Indian habitat," and "thus profoundly shapes their lives." At no place can we see this better and in all its complexity than at The Dalles. Two centuries ago, when white strangers first came to The Dalles, they found a place of extraordinary activity and enterprise. Here, where the river roared through the Long and Short Narrows, was the center of a vast trade network. What anthropologists have since come to call the Pacific-Plateau system involved exchanging huge quantities of dried salmon for other food and trade goods. Stretching from the Pacific Coast to Nez Perce homelands and linked to the Missouri River Indian villages by way of the Shoshoni Rendezvous, the network joined Chinookan- and Sahaptian-speaking peoples in an intricate set of personal and economic relationships. Through the trade system flowed not only fish, wappato bread, buffalo robes, and later European items, but also games, songs, and stories.

Geography, in the form of a dramatic narrowing of the Columbia at The Dalles and the resulting creation of ideal fishing stations, conspired with climate—warm, dry winds blowing up the Gorge—to make the Indian villages around the Narrows what explorer William Clark called "great marts of trade." Wishram Indians lived on the north bank at The Dalles; Wascos occupied sites on the south side of the river. Although trading and fishing took place from Celilo Falls down to The Dalles, the most intense bargaining was done at the main Wishram village. When Lewis and Clark visited the settlement in late October 1805, they found some twenty large wooden plank houses, each holding three extended families.

What no visitor could miss were the towering stacks of dried salmon. William Clark estimated that there were ten thousand pounds, pointing up the vast quantities of goods exchanged throughout the system. Trading took place from spring through fall, with most activity reserved for the fall season. During September and October, dried fish and roots were freshly prepared and in abundant supply. To The Dalles trade fair came nearby Yakama and Teninos as well as more distant Umatillas, Walulas, and Nez Perces. Local Sahaptins brought food products, including meat, roots, and berries. At the trading places, Wishram brokers exchanged these items for dried salmon and European cloth and ironware. Distant Sahaptins, especially the Nez Perces who had access to the plains, brought skin clothing, horses, and buffalo meat. Less interested in fish than their Columbia cousins, the Plateau people were drawn to the river in search of European goods, especially metal and beads.

Centered at The Dalles and with one arm stretching east, The Dalles river trade system also reached west down the Columbia to the coastal Chinookans. Pacific people used the river as a highway, bringing to The Dalles a variety of European goods obtained from maritime fur traders. Chinook canoes also carried indigenous food crops. Guns, blankets, clothing, and the prized blue beads—all came up the Columbia to The Dalles. Graceful canoes also transported wappato roots to be pounded and made into a tasty bread. Once at The Dalles, Chinookans traded for dried salmon, buffalo meat, and valuable bear grass used in making cooking baskets and the distinctive Northwest Coast hats.

The full flavor of a rendezvous at The Dalles must have been an unforgettable experience. The smell of dried fish hung in the fall air, and clouds of fleas and gnats hovered everywhere. At peak trading times, some three thousand Indians gathered for the rituals of bargain and exchange. But those festive fall days promised more than redistribution of wealth. Native people met old friends, made new ones, and heard the latest news. Gambling, socializing, and sporting for the opposite sex were all-important features of the trading days. Fur trader Alexander Ross, who saw The Dalles system before it was swept away by disease and white invasion, caught the spirit of those high times. "The Long Narrows," he wrote, "is the great emporium or mart of the Columbia and the general theatre of gambling and roguery."

Standing at The Dalles, any visitor—native or non-native—could see the visible signs of so vast a trading system. What was not so readily apparent in this river world was power and politics. On the Missouri, Teton Sioux bands gained and exercised power by controlling goods moving up and down the river. Upper Chinookans like the Skilloots did not have the military power possessed by the Tetons, but they were willing to resort to force to protect their accustomed place as river brokers, the middlemen on the Columbia. Just how far Indians from The Dalles to the Cascades would go to defend their role on the river would be revealed in 1812 and 1814, when river Indians fought pitched battles with fur traders for passage on the Columbia. Such was the contest of cultures as bearded strangers began to push and paddle their way into the Columbia River world.

For the native people of the big river, the Columbia was a fixed point in the rhythms of daily life. The river was there, in season and out. River spirits properly tended promised bounty and the security of a known place in a predictable world. Eighteenth century Europeans, of whatever national stripe, had a wholly different vision of the River of the West. In the geography of the mind, the Columbia was a ghost river, a fragment of the ever-elusive Northwest Passage. When gathered together, the fragments tell a story of empire and self-aggrandizement, national domain and personal ambition, communal pride and individual disappointment.

Robert Rogers is not a name quickly associated with the early history of the Columbia. This eighteenth century English soldier won his reputation in a series of bloody raids against pro-French Indians in northern New England. "Rogers' Rangers" brings to mind the shadowy world of irregular warfare, commandos, and Green Berets. But Robert Rogers was far more than a simple-minded frontier adventurer. In the mid-1760s, Rogers began to think long and hard about the rivers of North America. As he explained to English crown officials, he had a "great capacity for making Discoverys." In his mental geography of North America, Rogers imagined a single height of land, a continental divide, running north and south to split the country into two great watersheds. This bit of theoretical geography was not unique to Rogers. He probably borrowed it from French writers, but he was perhaps the first to give it expression in English. As Rogers envisioned it, one need only follow the Mississippi to its headwaters, cross the divide, and come upon the source of a mighty river bound for the Pacific. Rogers called this river the Ouragon. Following its path, English Americans could easily make their way to "the rich countries of the East." Here was the Northwest Passage and the dream of the China trade, a dream that would haunt the Columbia for generations to come.

Rogers's plea fared poorly, and in 1766 he was back in Massachusetts, planning his own transcontinental expedition. Rogers had just been appointed commander of the British garrison at Michilimackinac in the western Great Lakes. From that base, he intended to send a party up the Mississippi and on toward the Ouragon. His chosen adventurers were James Tute, former officer in the Rangers, and Jonathan Carver, lately mustered out of the provincial militia. The story of Carver's travels on the upper Mississippi in 1768 need not detain us. What is important is the book and map that came from his journals. In 1778, ten years after Carver's ill-starred search for the Ouragon, London booksellers offered a volume entitled *Travels through the Interior Parts of North America*. The first printing of the book contained a map showing the headwaters of the Ouragon somewhere within present-day North or South Dakota. Here was the big river, carrying in print for the first time the name Ouragon. In subsequent editions, Carver or his editor expanded the cartographic vision. The 1781 printing, appearing the year after Carver's death, holds a second landmark. That map offers the phrase "River of the West," located approximately where today's Columbia runs. That river strikes inland toward the empty space of the plateau. The Ouragon had become the River of the West.

But in telling you this I have taken you a bridge too far, a decade ahead of where we should be. Most of us would recognize 1792 as a pivotal year in Northwest history in general and Columbia River history in particular. But I would suggest that in the slippery world of dream and illusion, the year 1778 is far more important. That year held a trinity, a trio of events that would make the Columbia an imperial river, a highway for national domain. In London, it was Carver's book and map, announcing the Ouragon. Carver was joined that year by two of the most influential European explorers in Northwest history—Captain James Cook and fur-trade strategist Peter Pond. In the spring of 1778, Captain Cook was pressing his search for the Northwest Passage. Late May found his ships *Resolution* and *Discovery* along the Alaskan coast north of the Kenai Peninsula. There Cook found a tempting opening. The shape of the bay and the presumed river beyond it seemed to fit prevailing notions about the passage. After several days of probing, it seemed plain that this was not the true passage. But Cook was not so quick to abandon the illusion. He insisted that there was a river beyond the bay, that it stretched deep into the interior, and that someday it would be a great commercial highway. The illusory waterway soon carried the name Cook's River. It would not be until 1794 that Captain George Vancouver would end the illusion, giving Cook's Inlet its proper name and description.

At the same time that James Cook was chasing ghost rivers and fabled passages, fur trader and explorer Peter Pond crossed Methye Portage into the fur-rich Athabasca country of present-day northern Saskatchewan. Once in that country Pond heard from native people about rivers flowing west from Lake Athabasca to the sea. It was Columbus, Carver, and Cook revisited—the passage to the Orient. By 1784, Pond was certain that one of those rivers was the very one explored by Cook. Wintering at Athabasca in 1784 Pond began to draw a series of maps that expressed his western vision—that Lake Athabasca and the Great Slave Lake form a water hub for the entire Northwest. Pond imagined several rivers radiating, like spokes in a wheel, toward the north and the west. He was partly right. The Mackenzie, Peace, and Athabasca rivers do indeed head north and west from the lakes, but they do not make the navigable highway Pond and Cook so eagerly sought. Pond's 1785 map shows Cook's River heading inland from the Pacific while several Athabasca streams flow west to embrace it. In the early 1780s, Pond was uncertain about connections between the lakes and the western ocean. He easily confused Cook's River with the present-day Mackenzie. By 1789, wishful thinking had hardened to conviction. Cook's River was real, and it was the direct water route from the lakes to the sea.

At the end of the eighteenth century, Cook's River, the River of the West, and the Ouragon all ran together. Destiny's river was there because it had to be there. Europeans invented their Columbia before they saw it. As Barry Lopez reminds us in *Arctic Dreams*, desire and imagination create the landscape of the mind. Long before Robert Gray crossed the Bar and dropped anchor, Europeans were talking about the River of the West, dreaming it, scheming it, plotting its ways, and collecting its profits.

While we memorialize Gray and his crew as the initial European discoverers of the Columbia, the effective meaning of that discovery came from the creative mind of someone else. In so many ways, Alexander Mackenzie was the heir to the Carver-Cook-Pond legacy. The young Scot had wintered at Athabasca with Pond, and the old trader had taught his pupil the fundamentals of an imperial geography. After returning in 1794 from his great transcontinental trek to the Pacific, Mackenzie began to ponder the future of the Northwest. Although he initially confused the Columbia with the Fraser, by 1801 Mackenzie was quite convinced that the Columbia was the master river of the region. And he said so in unmistakable terms in his book *Voyages from Montreal*. Some historians have too quickly dismissed Mackenzie as an ambitious but parochial fur merchant, someone who never saw beyond stacks of pelts and lines in the ledgerbooks. But a careful look at Mackenzie and his writings reveals a far more interesting character and a vastly more complex vision. It was his vision of the river and the country around it that should now command our attention.

No one would ever accuse Mackenzie and his ghost writer William Combe of writing a compelling narrative. Even by the standards of the day, *Voyages from Montreal* was no page-turner. But for those who persevered—and among that company was Thomas Jefferson—the reward at the end of the book was geopolitical prophecy of the first water. "The Columbia," so proclaimed Mackenzie, "is the line of communication from the Pacific Ocean, pointed out by nature." The nation that controlled the Columbia, so it seemed, held the destiny of the entire region. For Mackenzie, the River of the West would carry more than a tide of pelts. Columbia's empire promised permanent white settlement, agricultural colonies to anchor Britain's western domain. Mackenzie said as much when he touted the region as "the most Northern situation fit for colonization, and suitable to the residence of a civilized people." In Mackenzie's imagination, the Columbia danced to the tune of trade, farming, and a revived British Empire. Only a few years before, the empire had lost destiny's other rivers—the Hudson, the Ohio, and the Mississippi. Now the empire might strike back and by winning the Columbia secure much of the far West.

But fortune and circumstance conspired in the first decade of the nineteenth century to delay and eventually defeat Mackenzie's Columbian enterprise. The idea of the Columbia as an imperial-industrial river was conceived in the enthusiastic imaginations of Rogers, Carver, and Pond, advanced by Mackenzie, and finally brought to full flower by Thomas Jefferson. Although the Sage of Monticello sometimes talked about himself as a savage of the American mountains, it was rivers that fascinated him. In his *Notes on the State of Virginia*, Jefferson filled page after page with vivid descriptions of those eastern rivers he knew and loved—the James, the York, and the Potomac. But there was more than an innocent literary Romanticism at work here.

Jefferson recognized the enduring political and economic significance of American rivers. They defined the country, gave it shape, and connected it to the wider world. By 1793, Jefferson had settled on the Columbia (or the Oregon as he sometimes called it) as his River of the West. It was not until the summer of 1802 that the Columbia became— at least for Jefferson—something more than a line on an Arrowsmith map. Reading Mackenzie's *Voyages from Montreal*, the president came to lines at the end of the book that were pure electricity. Here was the imperial challenge. Britain would plant an empire in the West, a domain along the Columbia. Mackenzie's vision now collided with Jefferson's. The president's dream of a republican empire of liberty was at risk. What Jefferson did over the next year is well documented in studies of the origins of the Lewis and Clark Expedition. By June 1803 Meriwether Lewis had comprehensive instructions from Jefferson for the first American probe of the West. Those instructions picked up and extended what other Euroamericans had said about the Columbia. What kind of a river was it to be? Jefferson's Columbia, like Mackenzie's, was to be an imperial highway. The river's mission and purpose was commerce and sovereignty. Virtually every other river dreamer after Jefferson would agree. The Columbia was all about fur, wheat, timber, railroads, tourists, and windsurfers.

No more than a decade after Jefferson spelled this out for Lewis and Clark, John Jacob Astor put a point on it in his usually blunt way. "The Columbia," he insisted, "is the key to a vast country." Astor saw the river carrying a current of furs and trade goods in a spacious commercial empire. Two decades later, Methodist missionary Henry Spaulding echoed Astor, saying that the river was the "keystone to the plain and mountainous country." In Spaulding's geography of faith, the river was predestined to carry gospel light into the heart of native darkness. The river as key to a vast country, whether for profit, power, or souls, had strong appeal among the ranks of government explorers, wheat farmers, mill owners, and steamboat captains. As Senator John H. Mitchell thundered in 1885, the Columbia was "the only real pass through which the productions of the Great Columbia plain can find their way to the seaboard." The river highway represented more than commerce. Mitchell made it a symbol of triumphant nationalism. The Columbia "was endowed with all those elements of greatness and grandeur and moral and physical power that constitute and characterize the greatest of the great internal waterways of the world." From the eighteenth century on, the river was defined more and more by the language of commerce and sovereignty. The course of the river ran through diplomatic offer and counteroffer and between ledgerbook lines. Fur-trade strategists, town planners, and transportation moguls all envisioned the Columbia as a trunk line, linking branch lines and way stations to great metropolitan market terminals.

We might well extend Columbia's chronology and waterscape from Fort Clatsop, Fort Astoria, and Fort Vancouver to Bonneville, Grand Coulee, and the Port of Portland. Those years defined the river space in a common way. The river world is the universe of energy and enterprise, dream and dominion. Historical geographer D. W. Meinig illuminates the ruling presence of the Columbia in his provocative book *The Great Columbia River Plain*. As Meinig explains it, the river and the region have gone through four distinct phases since the beginning of the nineteenth century. In the fur trade phase, the river tied the Columbia country east to Atlantic sources of investment capital, west to the China market, and north to the upper Columbia Canadian world. For missionaries, overland emigrants, soldiers, and miners, the Columbia was destination, pathway, and military corridor. Toward the end of the century, the river became a stream of wheat and cattle. The current that once carried fur, faith, and gold now ran heavy with grains like Spanish Little Club and Australian Bluestem. With the coming of various canal projects around The Dalles, and especially the railroads, the river entered what landscape historian John Stilgoe describes as "the engineered future." In the railroad age, the Columbia traffic-way was paved with the long steel rail and the short cross tie. The Columbia became what novelist Harold Waldo called a "river of steel." Henry Villard's imperial Oregon Railway and Navigation Company now bowed to competition from the Union Pacific on one side and the Spokane, Portland, and Seattle Railway on the other. "Uncle Pete" still rolls on the south side while the Burlington Northern hustles freight along the north bank. And in double-stacked container units marked APL, Mitsui O.S.K., and K-Line, the China trade has at last come to the Columbia. Today's passenger on Amtrak's *Pioneer* and *Empire Builder* is but following the iron path of countless travelers on premier trains like the *North Coast Limited*, *The Portland Rose*, and *The Columbia River Express*. Seen through Pullman windows or automobile windshields, the river was and remains just as much a commodity—scenery to be consumed and then held captive in an endless flow of postcards, snapshots, and fading memories.

A hundred and thirty-some years after Lewis and Clark, Woody Guthrie wrote a set of songs about the river and its future. Some of those songs have entered the folklore of the Northwest and at least one—"Roll On, Columbia"—seems destined to become the river's unofficial anthem. Today, Woody's poetry is cherished as a powerful evocation of the river's wonder and majesty. But before we hail Oklahoma's native son as the sweet singer of the Columbia, we might well pause to look carefully as the connections between the River of the West as defined by generations of promoters and entrepreneurs and Woody's own rolling Columbia. In three memorable songs—"Roll On, Columbia," "Grand Coulee Dam," and "Way Up in that Northwest"—Guthrie answered the question, what kind of a river is the Columbia. Or rather, what kind of river should it become. Putting himself squarely in the lineage of Mackenzie and Jefferson, Reverend Spaulding and Senator Mitchell, Guthrie wrote: "Tom Jefferson's vision would not let him rest / An empire he saw in the Pacific Northwest / Sent Lewis and Clark and they did the rest." What was the vision? What was the rest? In "Grand Coulee Dam," Guthrie offers an unmistakable answer: "Roll along, Columbia, you can ramble to the sea / But river, while you're rambling, you can do some work for me." The Columbia had once been, in Woody's words, a "wild and wasted stream." What tamed the river, made it useful and therefore beautiful, were the dams. "There at Bonneville on the river is a green and beautiful sight / See the Bonneville Dam arising in the sun so clear and white."* For Guthrie, the Dust Bowl of the Great Plains represented more than a regional nightmare and a personal disaster. The wind and dust seemed to challenge the very foundations of Jefferson's agrarian republic. How, Guthrie asked, could "dry barren hills" be transformed into "Green Pastures of Plenty" once again. The seemingly clean energy of hydroelectric force appeared the ideal solution. Dams and turbines would revitalize the American dream. Guthrie's industrial Columbia was not to be an oil-

---

*Lines from "The Grand Coulee Dam," words and music by Woody Guthrie, TRO © copyright 1958 (renewed) 1963 (renewed) 1976 Ludlow Music, Inc., New York, NY, reprinted with permission. Lines from "Roll On, Columbia," words by Woody Guthrie, music based on "Goodnight, Irene" by Huddie Ledbetter and John A. Lomax, TRO © copyright 1936 (renewed) 1957 (renewed) and 1963 (renewed) Ludlow Music Inc., New York, NY, reprinted with permission. Lines from "Way Up in That Northwest" by Woody Guthrie, copyright Woody Guthrie Publications, Inc., reprinted with permission.

stained, acid-laden river. The river could ramble and work at the same time. Perhaps this was the most persistent illusion in river history—that the Columbia could at once be changed and yet remain the same.

What we have thought about the Columbia—how we have defined the river by our plots and plans—reveals the larger stories of the Northwest and the continent. Long before the current crop of deep ecologists and their warnings against putting a human face on nature, James Agee offered the following:

> There is no need to personify a river: it is much too literally alive in its own way, and like air and earth themselves is a creature more powerful, more basic, than any living thing the earth has borne. It is one of those few, huge, casual and aloof creatures by the mercy of whose existence our own existence was made possible.

The living Columbia River has at one time or another appeared as a place to trade and fish, as a strategic center and zone of conflict, as a border and boundary, as a highway, as something to manipulate, as a destination, or as a passage to somewhere else.

What kind of a river is the Columbia? The voices answering that question are at once arrogant, optimistic, cranky, bitter, and painfully hopeful. Abigail Malick, riverfront homesteader, watched the Columbia flood her farm, "Sweaping every thing Before it." But as Lillian Schlissel reminds us in a sensitive essay about Abigail and her kin, the flood subsided and there was time to replant and run fence lines once more. Abigail's voice brings to mind Henry Van Dyke's pointed observation: "It is with rivers as it is with people: the greatest are not always the most agreeable nor the best to live with." As the river has flowed through our minds we have made it a barrier or a passage, a wild and wasted stream, or the fountain for a garden. The river is not the Other, some alien being or distant presence. We are not guilty of anthropomorphism by coming to believe that the river is the mirror of the Self, whether to shine or grow dark. What kind of a river the Columbia is, was, or might yet be depends on us—who we were, are, and might yet become.

Wendell Berry had it only partly right. The river is the ruling presence of the place. But now the river must share the ruling with the presence of human kind. And with all ruling comes obligation, the obligation to know the river's past and consider with care its future. We have not created the Columbia, but we have invented it. Invention imposes responsibility. In the ritual of the First Salmon, native people cared for the river. How can we express that same care for our invention? If it is true that the history of the river is the history of the soul, what does the Columbia reveal two hundred years after Robert Gray crossed the Bar?

"This perilous situation between hope and despair": Meetings along the Great River of the West

BY PATRICIA NELSON LIMERICK

There are four great rivers in the American West: the Missouri, the Rio Grande, the Colorado, and the Columbia. There are many more not-so-great rivers. From the point of view of white Americans, this was, in truth, the West's great weakness: most of its rivers were far too limited and variable in their flow. The idea of using most western rivers for navigation and commerce was, finally, laughable. Mark Twain spoke for many when he described the rivers of Nevada: "People accustomed to the monster mile-wide Mississippi grow accustomed to associating the term 'river' with a high degree of watery grandeur." When those people confront the Humboldt or the Carson, they learn "that a 'river' in Nevada is a sickly rivulet which is just the counterpart of the Erie Canal in all respects save that the canal is twice as long and four times as deep." But even these rivers had their uses: "One of the pleasantest and most invigorating exercises one can contrive is to run and jump across the Humboldt River until he is overheated, and then drink it dry."[1]

The Missouri, the Rio Grande, the Colorado, and the Columbia have, on occasion, defied the Euroamerican protocol for proper rivers, but they are undeniably great. Still, there has been some inequity of attention and respect toward these rivers. The Columbia has ten times the flow of the Colorado, and yet I suspect that the Colorado has had ten times more scholarly attention. Why? For the same reason that wild teenagers get more attention than hardworking teenagers. Freight transport has never been the Colorado River's strong suit. In the 1850s, when Lieutenant Joseph Christmas Ives tried to ascend the Colorado River in a steamboat, both the river and the local Indians mocked him. This was disheartening to Ives, because one of the reasons he had wanted to take a steamboat up the Colorado was to impress the Indians with the power of white people's technology. But as the boat struggled upstream, repeatedly running aground, Ives reported that Indians walked along the banks, laughing heartily and making frequent pauses to keep from getting ahead of the boat. The Colorado's resistance to working in the cause of white American settlement and development would not be broken by constructing a few portages; this was a river that had taken up a clear policy of defiance.

The Columbia, meanwhile, became a "working river" with less effort. While the Colorado River was still bouncing Major John Wesley Powell and his party around the rapids—scaring some so badly that they preferred to leave the river and court death by trying to climb out to the desert—and generating stories of romance, adventure, and untameability, the Columbia River had gone to work, and with only a few portages around the tough spots. Breaking the will of the rebellious Colorado with dams was a big and compelling story. Persuading the already steady and hardworking Columbia to work harder through hydroelectric dams seemed considerably less dramatic, and even expected and predictable.

The story of the Columbia River has been, in fact, just as dramatic and just as much worth a reckoning as the story of the Colorado. Benefit and cost, in this story, have intertwined to the point of inseparability. From 1860 to 1882, the Oregon Steam Navigation Company moved passengers and freight up and down the river and portaged around the Cascades and The Dalles, thus making the economic development of the subregion possible. The company ran a monopoly, and those who benefited from its services also had reason to resent the inflexible and steep rates they were charged. And so it went, costs and benefits in a veritable Maypole dance. The building of Grand Coulee Dam in the 1930s took nearly ninety human lives and made no accommodation for fish to go above the dam. The dam also produced an abundant flow of electricity, jobs, and irrigation water. The person who can separate out the good news from the bad news of that story has a much clearer eye than mine.

An encounter with the history of the Columbia River not only requires cautious judgment, it also makes one more alert to words and terms. Consider the very name, Columbia. The naming of the river rests on historical accident: in 1792, Captain Robert Gray was the first European or American to locate and enter the mouth of the river, and Captain Gray's ship was named the *Columbia Rediviva*. With a contingent chain of events naming the river and at the same time giving the United States its claim to the Pacific Northwest, the Columbia reminds us how odd and arbitrary the invaders' process of naming and claiming often was. One could not ask for a location more distant from the domain of Christopher Columbus, and yet the name Columbia drew the river into a direct and undeserved association with that controversial old admiral.

The arbitrariness of the river's name is not the only curious feature here. There is also a problem with Captain Gray himself. Over two hundred years ago, Gray crossed the Bar and made the first Euroamerican discovery of this great river. Instead of getting excited the captain barely seemed to notice. He returned instantly to the compelling business of looking for furs. Gray's affect, in the terms of current psychobabble, was distressingly low. We like our explorers to show a little more energy, maybe even exhilaration, in their written records. It is one thing to have a pilot's license or a captain's license, but people in Gray's position should also have been screened to make sure they carried a poetic license. If they did not qualify for that license, then they should not have been permitted to name rivers.

Many of the names in the Columbia's history carry this sense of Providence following a "truth in advertising" vow, bestowing names that sound as if a heavy-handed novelist picked them. Consider the captain of the *Tonquin*, J. J. Astor's employee Captain Jonathan Thorn—the cruel, dictatorial Captain Thorn, who fought and feuded his way to Astoria, who sacrificed eight of his men to inept efforts to cross the Columbia Bar, and who finally brought on his own destruction by mistreating Indians. The man's name is perfect; no Dickensian novelist could think of a better word than "thorn" to convey this man's sharp and unpleasant character. Or consider the daring involved in naming an enormous twentieth century power administration after a failed nineteenth century fur trader. The Bonneville Power Administration was named for a man who, in the 1830s, had failed in the Rocky Mountain and Northwest fur trade. In choosing this name, were the federal and state authorities saying, "Yes, we will name this network of dams after a known business failure," just as some people walk under ladders and court the company of black cats just to prove that they are not frightened of such things? If more challenges to ladders and black cats were needed, surely it was the height of linguistic defiance to make an enormous regional investment in an energy company with the acronym WPPS, or "whoops."

Consider another curious manifestation of Columbia-related verbal behavior. People writing about the Columbia River have often described the river as the great "artery" of the Pacific Northwest. Boosters and developers use this metaphor frequently. Yet, if the Columbia River is the region's artery, then there is only one meaning available within that metaphor for a dam. The Columbia River has become a very clogged artery, and the Army Corps of Engineers and the Bureau of Reclamation have been agents for the production, distribution, and installation of cholesterol, bringing the entire area to the verge of a major stroke.

Then there are the place names: Cape Disappointment, Deception Bay, and on and on. A map of the area is a vast mystery. How was it that the spirit of John Bunyan came back to govern the naming of the Pacific Northwest? Why does reading a map of this area become the equivalent of reading *Pilgrim's Progress*? Is Bunyan's Slough of Despond located on the coast, or somewhere near the Hanford Reach, or perhaps near the drowned Celilo Falls?

In the Pacific Northwest during the early nineteenth century, one troubled man spent more time than most of us do in the Slough of Despond. When the Astoria land party was struggling through the interior in 1811 and reached the neighborhood of present-day Lewiston, Idaho, "they came upon a man," as one participant described him,

> who was deranged, but who had some lucid moments. The young man told them, during one of his clearer intervals, that he was from Connecticut and that his name was Archibald Petton [Pelton]. He said that he had come up the Missouri with Mr. Henry and that the people at the trader's post had been massacred. He alone had escaped and had wandered for three years among the Indians.[2]

Pelton's story is incomplete, though it gives every indication of being very interesting. His mental problems were so conspicuous that local Indians took up his name and added it to the Chinook Jargon, the trade language of the Northwest. "Pelton" became an adjective meaning "foolish, crazy" and now appears in dictionaries for the Chinook Jargon. Pelton achieved a kind of immortality, with his surname preserved for the ages as a synonym for lunacy.[3]

There are different scales for measuring achievement and significance, but one cannot help thinking that poor Pelton, despite all his sufferings, did pretty well for himself. Anonymity is the cruelest historical fate of all, and Pelton escaped that, becoming an occasion of linguistic common ground, a term understood for a time by quite a number of Indians, French, British, and Americans. Originating as a form of intertribal communication when Northwest Indian people needed to talk to each other for trade or for purposes of common defense against enemies from the interior, the Chinook Jargon adopted and modified words from French and English. Broom became bloom, cry became cly, dry became dly, dollar became dolla or tahla, a quarter of a dollar became a kwahta, coffee became kaupy, paper became pehpah, and Pelton, of course, became pelton. Americans were Bostons, and Englishmen were King Chautsches, a reference to King George. A watch was a tiktik, a cat was a pusspuss. Laughter was tree tree, and a place of entertainment or amusement was a tree tree house. Many words in Chinook Jargon have clear English connections, though most of them are derived from local Indian languages. My favorite Chinook word is "hwah!" or "hwahwa!" an interjection denoting surprise or admiration. It is my favorite because "Hwah!" or "Hwah-wa!" is exactly what one feels like saying when contemplating Pelton, the Chinook Jargon, and the operations of the cultural borderland they both represent.[4]

There is no better device than this example of linguistic syncretism for showing the reality of the American West as a cultural borderland and meeting ground. When Lewis and Clark approached the Pacific Coast from the interior, they knew they were getting close to the ocean because the Indians started using European-derived words, some of them fairly off-color. History had come to life in the Pacific Northwest long before Anglo-American missionaries and settlers arrived on the scene.

The Columbia River country has long been a place of great cultural diversity and the site for exchanges that sometimes centered on conflict and sometimes on collaboration. Human encounters with nature and with other humans have been transactions of borders, occurring where zones of difference meet. The stories of natural borders and human borders can be equally compelling, and, in ways that western historians have not entirely mastered, those stories of borders, both human and natural, can inform and illuminate each other. Consider, for instance, the border between the sea and the land. In the case of the Columbia Bar, where a chain of sandbars created a terrifying place of passage, this is a point of intersection that makes the human/human encounters of the region look remarkably peaceful.

The Columbia River is, of course, not unique in having sandbars. The Platte, the not-so-great river of the Plains, also has sandbars, but they are dull, inconsequential pieces of matter compared to the dramatic sandbars at the mouth of the Columbia. There are a few tales of the Platte sandbars obstructing attempts to use the South Platte as a shipping tie to connect Denver to the Midwest, but those tales do more to amuse than to disturb.

In scale and power, the Columbia River is to the Platte what Superman is to Walter Mitty. And yet, thanks to its association with the Overland Trail, the Platte has been more intensely studied than the Columbia. We have books upon books about the people who traveled across the continent to reach the Pacific Coast. Bewitched by the tales of the Overland Trail, western American historians made an odd choice to pay little attention to the Pacific Ocean as a route of approach to western America. Plenty of people went to the California gold fields by ship, yet the term "California Gold Rush" uniformly brings to mind images of people traveling by wagon and pack train. Everyone recognizes the names Lewis and Clark, but the maritime equivalents of those explorers—Gray, Vancouver, Broughton, Slacum, Wilkes, Howison—hover on the distant, shrinking edges of name recognition. I am not standing at a distance and condemning others for a limited historical vision from which I have been exempt. I have pondered Lewis and Clark's journals lots of times, but only recently did I read the logs and journals from the Broughton, Slacum, Wilkes, and Howison expeditions. Why did I submit to a moratorium on maritime curiosity? Without any conscious thought, I had acted on the accurate understanding that if I had not read the journals of Lewis and Clark, I would be universally recognized as a dummy in western American circles. If I had not read Slacum or Wilkes, nobody would notice or care. Why? Here is one possibility. We have favored overland travel because it provides narratives with a more bearable level of vicarious anxiety. Following along with Lewis and Clark can be suspenseful and even agonizing, especially when the party is struggling to cross the Rockies and find the headwaters of the Columbia. Their trip along the Missouri and through the Rockies is full of discomfort: prickly-pear spines in the feet, constant exertion, precarious mountain paths, hunger, disorientation. And yet, while the story is emotionally strenuous, it is not terrifying. Land, and even the rivers that cut through land, offer a kind of predictability and manageability that the ocean refuses to provide. Lewis and Clark would have understood the contrast I am drawing here. Clark's wonderful notation from December 1, 1805, is as agitated and unsettled in sentiment as it is in grammar:

The emence Seas and waves which breake on the rocks & Coasts to the S W. & N W roars like an emence fall at a distance, and this roaring has continued ever Since our arrival in the neighborhood of the Sea Coast which has been 24 days Since we arrived in Sight of the Great Western; (for I cannot say Pacific) Ocian as I have not Seen one pacific day Since my arrival in its vicinity, and its waters are forming and petially [perpetually] breake with emenc waves on the Sands and rocky Coasts, tempestuous and horiable.[5]

Here, I think, Clark was saying in effect, "Meriwether Lewis and I could deal pretty well with the challenges of travel by land and river, but this damned Pacific is something else entirely."

For a latter-day reader, an Overland Trail narrative of exploration or settlement has a bearable level of tension and suspense. There are steep hills to climb and descend, there are sometimes alarming variations of weather, and there is the ongoing anxiety about finding grass and water for the animals. There is, indeed, a chance that the person whose fate the reader is following might die, but there is a much better chance that she or he will live.

The narratives from the other direction, told by the explorers trying to enter present-day Oregon from the sea, offer no such comfort. Even when one is reading a narrative two hundred years old, the tension can be unbearably high. The vicarious suspense is neither adventurous nor fun, and one cannot dismiss the chances of sudden and agonizing death. The conditions of shipboard society add to the tension. Parties of overland travelers could get on each other's nerves and tear into each other psychologically in riveting ways. Still, there is something about life confined to a small ship, with all the frictions of command, hierarchy, and class, that can make a shipboard society into something dangerous as psychological fuel and tinder. No wonder, then, that we have kept our eyes and attention focused on the land.

At the Columbia Bar, between Cape Disappointment and Point Adams, a huge and powerful river meets a vast and agitated ocean. The river deposited sediment at its mouth, forming a shifting and changeable line of sandbars. Waves, tides, currents, winds, and the pouring force of the river created a navigational puzzle beyond the mastery of many navigators. Consider the report of Lieutenant Neil M. Howison, who entered the Columbia on July 1, 1846, explored the river, and then tried to depart on September 10. Howison had with him a description of the Bar and a guide to its navigation written by American explorer Charles Wilkes, who had crossed the Bar in 1841. But those instructions were of mixed value. These sandbars were under no contract to hold still, and five years had passed since Wilkes had written his description. "[T]he sands about the mouth of the Columbia," Howison reported, "had undergone great changes within a short time past, . . . which made it impossible to enter the river by the old marks, or those laid down on Wilkes's chart." These new formations, Howison said, "greatly obstructed this already embarrassing navigation, and those most experienced—undertook to cross the bar with apprehension and dread." [6] Why was Howison so careful to report on the problems of the Bar? On September 10, 1846, when he tried to leave the Columbia, "the attempt was made and resulted in the shipwreck of the schooner." Howison and his party found themselves "cast on shore . . . with nothing besides the clothes we stood in, and those thoroughly saturated." [7]

Howison's accident reminds us of the curious patterns of fortune in western history. A number of early mariners "failed" in discovery by missing the mouth of the Columbia as they sailed along the coast. While this may have been unlucky in terms of reducing their future fame as explorers, there was also considerable luck in their escape from Howison's fate. Finding the Columbia River required a mariner to challenge the Bar, both coming and going. On that count, missing the perilous mouth of this river could easily be counted as good fortune, not bad.

In 1792, British explorer George Vancouver headed north along the coast and also missed the mouth of the river. In May, after Vancouver had passed, Captain Robert Gray discovered the river and successfully crossed the Bar. In October, after encountering Gray, hearing his news, and getting some advice Vancouver headed south along the coast. Vancouver was going to give the Columbia another try. His subordinate,

Lieutenant William Robert Broughton, crossed the Bar and took his smaller vessel, the *Chatham*, at least a hundred miles up the river.

Broughton had with him a sketch drawn by Gray that was supposed to locate the channels that would permit a safe passage across the Bar. But those channels were very shallow, and having a sketch in hand was no protection against misadventure or panic. A participant in the Broughton expedition described this dreadful crossing:

> I must here acknowledge that in going into this place, I never felt more alarmed and frightened in my life, never having been in a situation where I conceived there was so much danger. The Channel was narrow, the water very Shoal, and the Tide running against the Wind at the rate of 4 Knots an hour, raised a Surf that broke entirely around us, and I am confident that in going in, we were not twice the Ship's length from Breakers, that had we struck on, we must inevitably have gone to pieces, without the most distant hope of a single life being saved.

But the Broughton party was lucky, and the *Chatham* proceeded upriver. Even though Broughton tried to follow Captain Gray's sketch, he soon found it unreliable: "following the track of the Soundings laid down in the Sketch we shoal'd our water considerably in a few Casts of the Lead, and before we could wear round, the Vessel struck on a Sand Bank." They freed themselves from that sandbar, but proceeded with great caution, with "the Navigation of this River being found so intricate and the Sketch of Mr. Grey's so little to be depended upon."[8]

In November, when the Broughton party tried to leave the river and return to the sea, the terrors of the Bar proved to be just as great as when they had approached from the sea. As they contemplated their departure, "the late bad weather had caused such a dreadful Swell over the Shoals at the entrance that we could observe no Channel free from Breakers." They waited several days, and then, with the channel appearing "tolerably smooth," they set out. The passage seemed to go well, "but we had scarce pass'd the Bar, when a tremendous Surf appeared rolling towards us, and broke over the Vessel with great violence, the Spray of it when it struck us, wetted the Foresail as high as the upper reef, the Main Deck was filled with Water fore and aft." Their escape was, again, a narrow one:

> Had we not had the Ship's head to these Seas at the time they broke, there is little doubt but we must either have been lost, or have had all our Masts carried away, and even as it was, had not the precaution of battening down the Hatches been taken, we must have imminently endangered ourselves by the quantity of Water she would have taken in.[9]

For one man, the terror of the passage must have exceeded anything we can imagine. As it crossed the Bar, the *Chatham* was towing a cutter, a twenty-foot-long open boat, which successfully "rose to the Seas." The cutter, in turn, was towing a launch with one man in it. "[B]y the sudden violent motion of the Vessel and the force of the Sea, [the launch] broke her Tow rope, which was a stout Hawser of four Inches, and instantly fill'd." The others could do nothing to help: "we were in the greatest anxiety for a while about the poor fellow . . . , for we could not yet venture to send the Cutter to [the launch's] assistance, till we were ourselves clear of all dangers." When the rescuers could finally act, the launch's solitary passenger, miraculously, proved to be safe, though "everything belonging" to the boat, "Oars, Masts, Sails, was lost and her side was stove in." This was not the end of the *Chatham*'s encounter with maritime terror. Sailing south along the Oregon coast, the party continued to be battered and shaken, losing sails and anchors to squalls and gales.[10]

For people like me, these Columbia Bar stories are close to unbearable. I do not read suspense novels, and I do not watch suspense movies. At a certain level of desperate, vicarious tension, I feel more agonized than entertained. I do not want to begin to imagine the experience of the fellow alone in that little launch, on his own in huge and clashing seas, while his boat disintegrated around him. At least in this case, there is the heartening and consoling ending of a life saved, even if saved more by miracle than human skill. In the literature of the Columbia Bar, however, such a happy ending is by no means assured.

Consider the arrival of the maritime half of the Astoria party in 1811. The people on board the *Tonquin*, commanded by the cruel Captain Thorn, were happy to see land. "The sight filled every heart with gladness," Alexander Ross wrote. Omens to interrupt that gladness appeared instantly as "the cloudy and stormy state of the weather prevented us seeing clearly the mouth of the river." The party could see clearly that the aspect of "the coast was wild and dangerous."[11]

Captain Thorn sent out an exploratory party to examine the channel. In the party were the officer Mr. Fox, with "one sailor, a very old Frenchman, and three Canadian lads, unacquainted with sea service—two of them being carters from La Chine, and the other a Montreal barber." Fox was reluctant to go. He declared "the impossibility of performing the business in such weather, and on such a rough sea, even with the best seamen, adding, that the waves were too high for any boat to live in." Alexander Ross described Thorn's response to Fox's protest: "The captain, turning sharply round, said—'Mr. Fox, if you are afraid of water, you should have remained at Boston.'" Thus challenged, Fox departed with a melancholy farewell to his friends.[12] "The weather was boisterous, and the sea rough," but Fox's fellow sailers could see enough to know that before his boat had gone far "she became utterly unmanageable. . . . At last she hoisted the [white] flag; the meaning could not be mistaken; we knew it was a signal of distress." It was a signal to which Captain Thorn chose not to respond. That was the last heard of Mr. Fox, the sailor, the old Frenchman, the two carters, and the Montreal barber.[13]

In another reconnaissance, following the loss of Mr. Fox and his party, Ross traveled in a longboat to explore the channel. He described the Bar vividly:

> On approaching the bar, the terrific chain of breakers, which kept
> rolling one after another in awful succession, completely overpow-
> ered us with dread; and the fearful suction or current became so ir-

resistibly great, that, before we were aware of it, the boat was drawn into them, and became unmanageable.

The party strained to retreat, "for twelve minutes struggling in this perilous situation, between hope and despair, before we got clear."[14]

This, of course, was only a preliminary try at the channel. On the morning of March 25, a party went out in the longboat to "discover if possible the proper channel." With the longboat traveling ahead, Captain Thorn followed, taking the *Tonquin* itself into the passage. When the waves became wilder, Thorn refused to retrieve the men in the longboat, telling those who protested that he would "not endanger the ship" to rescue the longboat party. As the channel became more and more shallow, the people on board the *Tonquin* had their own dose of terror: "the surges breaking over her stern overwhelmed everything on deck. Everyone who could, sprang aloft, and clung for life to the rigging."

> The waves at times broke ten feet high over her, and at other times she was in danger of foundering; she struck again and again, and, regardless of her helm, was tossed and whirled in every direction, and became completely unmanageable. . . . Our anxiety was still further increased by the wind dying away, and the tide still ebbing. At this instance, some one called out, "We are all lost, the ship is among the rocks."

By throwing out the anchors, the men were able to slow down the drift of the ship toward the rocks and to arrive "in safety" at Baker's Bay. This was safety, of course, only for those on board the *Tonquin*. It was something quite different for those who had been passengers on the abandoned longboat. During the next days, the men from the *Tonquin* found only two survivors. Ross reported that "eight men in all lost their lives in entering this fatal river."[15]

In this story of the Bar, it is hard to tell which element is more awful: the clashing of natural elements, or the clashing of human character on board the *Tonquin*. "Mr. Fox, if you are afraid of water, you should have remained at Boston." It is hard to re-read that line without wanting to suggest that Mr. Fox, this time, turn back to Captain Thorn and say, "Mr. Thorn, of this water, any sensible man would be afraid. I had no reason to stay in Boston, but I have very good reason to stay on board this ship."

These moments of attempted cross-chronological intervention come, I am forced to confess, more and more to me. They are like those moments when small children or elderly people with Alzheimer's speak to the television as if the people on TV could hear them. The Columbia River country particularly brings those moments out in me. I yearn to tell Hudson's Bay Company Chief Factor John McLoughlin that he will have to be very careful in his dealings with these American intruders. I strain to tell Narcissa Whitman that she really ought to look into the possibilities of church work closer to home in New York and leave the Cayuse to their own choices. I struggle to tell Mr. Fox to stand his ground and refuse to be baited into sacrificing himself and his five companions. These are peculiar moments, and by a certain cult of historical objectivity, they are very bad moments, moments for which I should apologize. And yet, worse than refusing to apologize, I feel inclined to ask teachers of history at every level to encourage this urge to telephone, FAX, or e-mail across the centuries. If we licensed our students to give free play to this powerful urge, present in nearly everyone, to respond to the dilemmas of people in trouble, we would do a great deal to engage young people in the study of history, even though they are members of a generation that is not overwhelmed with enthusiasm for this enterprise. The worst thing we can do to historical figures is to convey the sense that they were not fully human, not fully alive in their moment, not, in other words, worth mourning.

So, by all means, mourn Mr. Fox. By all means, imagine what one could have done to save him and that poor, youthful, martyred Canadian barber who accompanied him. We are a couple of centuries late to be helpful, but it is still good exercise for the emotions and for the historical imagination to forget, for a moment or two, that one has been born too late to keep Mr. Fox out of those punishing and murderous waves and to give it a try anyway.

When one thinks what one would say to William Slacum, another early crosser of the Columbia Bar, it is hard to get beyond "Good heavens." Slacum's encounter with the Bar seems, at first, to have been a tranquil one, though, on reflection, it may have been the most violent of all. In 1836, President Andrew Jackson asked William Slacum "to obtain some specific and authentic information in regard to the inhabitants of the country in the neighborhood of the Oregon or Columbia River." Slacum, like Gray, was not an expressive fellow. Even when the federal government declined to repay him for many of his traveling expenses, he seemed more calm than crazed. He recorded his crossing of the Columbia Bar with little excitement. "We attempted the passage at twelve M.," he reported, "and crossed the bar safely, in not less than five fathoms, and anchored, at two o'clock, in Baker's bay." [16]

For all the apparent uneventfulness of his crossing, Slacum was aware of the problem that the Bar posed for American commerce: "At present, vessels are kept outside for several days waiting for clear weather to run in, having neither beacon, buoys, nor lights to guide them when close in with the shore." But Slacum was an optimistic and confident man. "This delay," he wrote, "would be obviated in a great measure if the coast was surveyed and properly lighted." Slacum's vision of the human capacity to master a natural obstacle, however, went way beyond maps and warning lights. His plan focused on Cape Disappointment, on the northern side of the mouth of the river. Cape Disappointment, Slacum wrote,

> is a high, bold promontory, about 400 feet above the sea, covered with timber from its base to the top. . . . I cannot leave this subject without pointing out the great facility and the advantages that would result from a thorough cut of not more than three-quarters of a mile through the lowest point of Cape Disappointment, from Baker's bay to the ocean. The soil is light, and the height not more than sixty feet at the point proposed; and I have not the slightest doubt that a deep and safe channel would soon be made by the

> action of the tide . . . as it sweeps around the bay, bringing with it
> the whole volume of water of the Columbia and its tributaries.[17]

Maybe, in 1836, the technology of explosives was further advanced than I realize. Maybe blasting a cut three-quarters of a mile long, seventy or eighty feet deep, through solid earth, was easily within the grasp of the engineers and artisans of the 1830s. Maybe I am doing Slacum a disservice by seeing a flaw in his thinking. If sediment deposited by the Columbia River formed the sandbars that made the present mouth such a navigational nightmare, what would stop the sediment from accumulating in this new, engineered channel?

Even if I am underestimating or misunderstanding Slacum here, his thoughts are nonetheless astonishing. Solve the problem of the Columbia Bar by blasting through Cape Disappointment? This sounds exactly like the fevered dreams proposed in the 1950s by Operation Plowshare and by advocates of atomic energy such as Edward Teller. This seems to be a match for the Plowshare plans to use atomic bombs to remove poorly placed mountains, to blast shipping channels to remote Alaskan ports, to pulverize oil shale in Colorado. There was William Slacum, in 1836, sounding like an employee of the Atomic Energy Commission or the Department of Energy and telling us that there really is a strong streak in American culture of boundless faith in technology to tidy up a messy and ill-designed physical world.

Slacum did not get his Cape Disappointment canal, although two enormous jetties and occasional bouts of channel-dredging have reduced some of the terror of the Columbia Bar. In his fine book on the Columbia River, Sam McKinney remarked that the Bar has, over two centuries, "claimed over two thousand boats and ships, and at least fifteen hundred lives." In a compelling chapter in *Reach of Tide, Ring of History*, McKinney visited the Columbia River Bar Pilots Association. There he found specialists in guiding ships over the Bar, men who had learned to take a terrifying leap of faith when they cross, in high seas, from a tugboat to a ship in need of guidance. McKinney also profiles people at the United States Coast Guard Station, set up in 1880 to save lives along the Bar. In the winter months, when mostly commercial boats are in operation, the station averages "150 requests for assistance." In the summer, as recreational sportfishing boats head out to the sea, the reqests for help increase. In one thirty-day period in the summer, the station recorded "three hundred distress calls," one every 2.4 hours by McKinney's calculations. When conditions are rough, the Coast Guard asks boaters to wait before crossing the Bar. Some boaters, McKinney writes, "interpret the closure as a curtailment of their liberties" and attempt to cross anyway, always to their peril and sometimes to their death. This border, where river meets ocean and humans meet the strongest forces of the planet, remains untamed.[18]

The American West is a borderland, and one definition of that borderland appears in the Chinook Jargon, where words from very different origins met and merged and where Archibald Pelton became an adjective for battiness. Another definition of the American West as borderland appears at the Columbia Bar, where land meets ocean, where the Great River of the West meets the Great Ocean of the West. The challenge facing western American historians in the 1990s is to put those borderlands—the natural and the human—into some relationship to each other. What I am referring to here is the well-established separation between environmental history and ethnic history. Many historians write about the encounter of diverse groups in the American West, and many historians write about the encounter between humans and the physical environment. With few exceptions, these are two different groups of historians, two groups who do not often talk to each other.

Then, in more practical and contemporary terms, some activists work on the question of how we will ever achieve social justice, how we will ever arrive at a social system of equality, fairness, and tolerance. Others work on the question of how we will achieve environmental balance and repair, how we will ever arrive at an environmental system of permanence, stability, and long-range health. While there are a few movements to tie these concerns together, these efforts are still very separate and social justice and environmental justice often seem unrelated or, worse, actively opposed.

We do something helpful every time we try to bring these matters back together. These stories had better connect, or the peril for future generations is enormous. Every time we try to keep the story of the relations between humans and nature in the same picture as the story of the relations between and among humans themselves, we are doing something useful. For the Columbia country, the sources make this easy.

Remember William R. Broughton who, as a part of George Vancouver's expedition, followed Gray into the Columbia and made a considerably more extensive reconnaissance? In Broughton's experience, the ties between the Columbia Bar as natural border and the Indian/white encounter as cultural border are instantly in place. Broughton had barely moved into the river when he encountered natives. His party soon reached the site of a deserted village—whether deserted by choice or by depopulation from European-introduced diseases, it does not seem possible to tell. Just three days after Broughton crossed the Bar, "one very large Canoe with about five and twenty Indians in her . . . came along side and brought some Salmon which we eagerly bought of them on reasonable terms; they also brought two or 3 Otter Skins for sale and seem'd to know the value of them very well." From that point on, the Broughton party was in constant contact with Indians. The sailors were, it is important to note, jumpy about this, trying to keep the Indians at some distance at night, guarding their onshore camp, and constantly staying alert to occasions of theft. In their efforts to keep the Indians at a distance, the Broughton party made this business of borders very concrete and literal. On one evening, with two hundred and fifty Indians in the area, one member of Broughton's party reported: "when we landed we drew a line on the Beach, at the same time giving them to understand that we did not wish them to come within it, which they punctually observed."[19]

For all this line-drawing, the spirit of the encounter seems to have been more amiable than hostile. After a visit from Indian men who "behaved very civilly," the party "found one of our drinking Potts had been march'd off with, but of this we took no notice willing to keep peace with them, even at the expense of a trifling theft." When a group of Indian men in "war Garments" approached, the situation had the potential to be explosive. The English

> regulated every thing in the best manner for our defense, the Swivel was primed, and a Match kept burning, all the Muskets and Pistols in the two boats were loaded with Ball, and every man had his Cartouch Box buckled on him, with his musket by his side, together with a Cutlass, Pistols, &c.

The Indians had a good set of bows and arrows, and it looked as if all the pieces were in place for a 1792 version of "Mutually Assured Destruction." Yet, the outcome proved to be quite different. "Soon after this," the report continued, "perceiving that our intentions were as peaceable, as their own, they took off all their War Garments and every man seem'd eager to dispose of his Bows and Arrows for old Buttons, Beads, &c." Throughout their time in the river, trade with the Indians also kept the Broughton party from hunger: "what with Venison, Wild Fowl & Salmon which the natives brought us in abundance" along with "large quantities of excellent Cranberries, we contrived to live tolerably well." [20]

There is no question here, or in any other record of exploration, that the ties between the European encounter with nature and the European encounter with Indian people were very close. The people of the past did not separate these experiences into two intact categories, natural and human. It is distinctly odd that academic historians have chosen to divide a historical topic that came to us whole.

The issues of human affairs and natural affairs are tied together in innumerable ways. In 1844, the confident and optimistic explorer John C. Frémont made a clear and unmuddled judgment of the political significance of the Columbia River. Frémont could make no claims to discovering the Columbia, but he did, in his usual manner, offer a forceful summation of the river's meaning for national destiny. The Atlantic Coast, he explained, was a very different geographical matter, with many rivers opening "many lines of communication with the interior." But the Columbia, Frémont wrote, "is the only river which traverses the whole breadth of the country, breaking through all the ranges, and entering the sea." The Columbia "opens the way into the interior of the continent," and that "fact," Frémont thought, "gives an immense value to the Columbia."

> Its mouth is the only inlet and outlet to and from the sea; . . . it is therefore the only line of communication between the Pacific and the interior of North America; and all operations of war or commerce, of national or social intercourse, must be conducted upon it. This gives it a value beyond estimation, and would involve irreparable injury if lost.

The Columbia would thus give Americans control, since only one nation would hold both coast and interior. The very structure of the coast, Frémont thought, would deepen that control. The coast was "what the seamen call *iron bound*." It was "high and compact, with few bays, and but one that opens into the heart of the country." This rugged, impenetrable coast, Frémont said, "gives to the country an immense military strength, and will probably render Oregon the most impregnable country in the world."[21]

Reading this passage a century and a half later, we cannot escape noticing that Frémont's assumptions make a striking contrast to our own. Frémont believed that danger, peril, and threat to the United States would come from outside. In his vision, American citizens would plant themselves on the coast and incorporate the Oregon Country into a healthy and thriving republic. As Americans fronted the Pacific, the geography of the coast and of the Columbia would protect them from outside threats and enemies.

One hundred and fifty years later, Frémont's assumptions are directly reversed. It is not simply a matter of the decimation of the salmon runs by the installation of dams in the river or of the many heated social conflicts triggered by that dilemma. The worst story of peril along the Columbia is the story of the Hanford Nuclear Reservation. In 1943, as part

of the Manhattan Project, the federal government built plutonium production facilities next to the Columbia, where the operations could
benefit from both abundant cooling water and hydroelectric power.
Careful waste management was never Hanford's strong suit. Over the
years, responding to Cold War pressures for increased nuclear arma-
ments, the Hanford Reservation produced chemical and radioactive
waste and plutonium. Dumped into waste pits, into improvised holding tanks, and into the Columbia itself, contaminated waste saturated
Hanford and polluted the river. Both downstream and downwind from
Hanford, a host of Americans stricken by cancer have lived with the un-
happy puzzle of wondering if their illness was a side-effect of the Cold
War prescription for national security.

Frémont, this miserable foundation for hindsight permits us to say,
got it wrong. The threat did not come from outside. The enemy was not
a set of invading foreigners, and no one tried to storm that "iron bound"
coast. A rocky, unapproachable coast could not protect Americans from
themselves. The enemy, as it turns out, came from the other direction;
and the enemy, as Pogo put it, was us. The national pursuit of what Frémont called "an immense military strength" proved to be exactly the
problem. Instead of becoming "the most impregnable country in the
world," the Columbia country became one of the most vulnerable. The
perils of the Columbia Bar begin to look more manageable in compari-
son to the perils we have created for ourselves.

During the nineteenth century, when Europeans and Euroamericans
tried to cross the Bar, they often turned to Indian pilots, to the people
who had the best knowledge of the shifting currents and bars. A professional pilots association still assists ships in making the transition from
sea to river. "The constant alterations," Lieutenant Neil Howison wrote
in 1846, "which this bar, in common with most others, is undergoing, go
to prove the necessity of frequent surveys and the establishment of resident pilots, who can be constantly exploring the channel, and keep pace
with the shifting of sands, and the consequent change in the direction of
the tides."[22]

This quotation virtually demands that we take it as an analogy and a metaphor. Without much effort from the interpreter, Howison's words translate directly from the Columbia Bar to the complicated human and environmental relations of our time. In race relations and in environmental conflicts and dilemmas, we are today as much in need of the services of "resident pilots" as seamen like Howison were in the 1840s. Indeed, this seems to be the happiest and most productive way of defining the role of teachers and writers of history in the American West today. We must be people who keep our eyes on the changing and treacherous obstacles and barriers that divide groups and individuals from each other. The situation of urgency in these matters matches the urgency that still confronts people crossing from the sea into the Columbia River. In "this perilous situation between hope and despair," resident pilots still have lives to save.

NOTES

1. Mark Twain, *Roughing It* (1872; reprint, New York: New American Library, 1962), 159.

2. Gabriel Franchère, *Adventure at Astoria, 1810–1814*, ed. and trans. Hoyt C. Franchère (Norman: University of Oklahoma Press, 1967), 67. See also Ross Cox, *The Columbia River*, ed. Edgar I. Stewart and Jane R. Stewart (Norman: University of Oklahoma Press, 1957), 60; and J. Neilson Barry, "Archibald Pelton, the First Follower of Lewis and Clark," *Washington Historical Quarterly* 19 (November 1928): 199–201.

3. George Gibbs, *Alphabetical Vocabulary of the Chinook Language* (New York: Cramoisy Press, 1863); Chester Anders Fee, "Oregon's Esperanto—the Chinook Jargon," *Oregon Historical Quarterly* 19 (November 1920): 176–85.

4. Ibid.

5. Gary E. Moulton, ed., *The Journals of the Lewis and Clark Expedition*, vol. 6 (Lincoln: University of Nebraska Press, 1990), 104.

6. "Report of Lieutenant Neil M. Howison on Oregon, 1846," *Oregon Historical Quarterly* 14 (March 1913): 4.

7. Ibid., 10.

8. J. Neilson Barry, ed., "Columbia River Exploration, 1792," *Oregon Historical Quarterly*, pt. 1, 26 (March 1927): 34–6.

9. Ibid., pt. 2, 26 (June 1927): 148–50.

10. Ibid., 149–50.

11. Alexander Ross, *Adventures of the First Settlers on the Oregon or Columbia River, 1810–1813* (Lincoln: University of Nebraska Press, 1986), 76.

12. Ibid., 76–7.

13. Ibid., 77.

14. Ibid., 79.

15. Ibid., 79, 81–2, 85.

16. "Slacum's Report on Oregon, 1836–1837," *Oregon Historical Quarterly* 13 (June 1935): 175.

17. Ibid., 182, 199.

18. Sam McKinney, *Reach of Tide, Ring of History* (Portland: Oregon Historical Society Press, 1987), 9, 30–1.

19. Barry, ed., "Columbia River Exploration," pt. 1, 39; pt. 2, 144.

20. Ibid., pt. 1, 41, 42; pt. 2, 143–4, 149.

21. Donald Jackson and Mary Lee Spence, eds., *The Expeditions of John Charles Frémont*, vol. 1 (Urbana: University of Illinois Press, 1970), 699–700.

22. Howison, "Report," 16.

"They have no father,
and they will not mind me":
Families and the River

BY LILLIAN SCHLISSEL

$\mathcal{A}$s an easterner writing western history, I know the region does not reveal itself easily to strangers. Like a honky-tonk town, the West hides its
darker streets. As a historian of women's lives, I know that women, east
and west, do not always come forward with their own realities. But then,
historians have not always looked for those realities. When I began collecting the writings of women who were part of the overland migration
of the 1840s and 1850s, few historians considered women's writings significant. Women offered anecdotal evidence, sentimental excess, recipes,
and assorted trivia, not the "hard" evidence of cut-offs and Indian skirmishes. But the question kept recurring: if a familiar event like the overland migration were told entirely through the eyes of women, would it
change what we already knew? Would women provide new data or alter
the conformation of the event we thought we so thoroughly understood?
And I began to gather the diaries and journals and letters of over a hundred women. After six years reading the fragmentary snatches of wom-
en's writings, I was convinced that the stories *were* different. For one
thing, women tried to hold the family together while men stretched
the family like a rubber band until it reached the new lands. Women

wrestled against uprooting while men assumed family was like a weed—pull it up, and it would grow again anywhere you set it. There were distinctly different views of the journey women and men made together.

In *Women's Diaries of the Westward Journey*, I wrote about "anonymous" women, part of the overland journey because their husbands or fathers had made the decision to go. These women understood the need, but they had not chosen the journey. With their men, they hoped for a better life, a new home, a chance for the children, all those human aspirations historians translate into statistical data: income, acreage, crops, agriculture, mining, ranching. But for women, changing the direction of history meant the chaos of kids who get the measles and poison ivy and of families with dysentery and cholera. Most historians are trained to look for order, for beginnings and ends, for cause and effect. But ordinary life is a muddle, and women's writing brings one up close to the disorder of journeys that end with wagons left on the road; horses, oxen, and cows dead in the mountains; mothers riding into the territory on mules; and small children strapped front and back to the saddles or soaking wet on rafts guided by Indians. These are stories you all know, and hardship is an assumed experience of pioneering. But do such details change history?

For one thing, women's writing frames new issues. Between the ages of fifteen and thirty-five, women were in their childbearing years; and while men of the same age were braced for the challenges of new lands, women could not have been prepared for childbirth in moving wagons or in wet tents or for a journey that could not be halted. They could not have been prepared for the cholera that swept through wagon parties between 1851 and 1853 or for burying their dead in unmarked graves on an unsurveyed landscape. Since care of the sick and the dying was "women's work," these experiences marked women's journeys in profound ways. Women confronted the human costs of uprooting and, in their own ways, questioned what westering was all about. They seldom wrote about conquest and felt themselves survivors more than heroes. Helped by Indians who traded food and brought them across rivers, women thought of themselves as lucky to be alive.

When *Women's Diaries of the Westward Journey* was published in 1982, I felt I had an unfinished story.[1] What happened to those new settlers of the Willamette Valley? What kind of life did they find? *Far From Home*, published in 1989, contains the stories of three families who went West to find a better life.[2] The first of three, the Malicks, came into the Oregon Territory in 1848. George Malick's people were German Lutherans who arrived in America in the 1700s and stood fast with George Washington at Valley Forge. Abigail was a Stuart who believed her family was descended from the royal line of England. They were part of the British East India Company. Abigail and George married and farmed near Lancaster, Pennsylvania, in the 1820s. In the 1830s, with three children, they moved on to Illinois. Their eldest daughter married into a family named Albright and soon had children of her own. In 1848, George and Abigail Malick decided that "moving on" was their American birthright, and they set out for Oregon. The Albrights promised that the following season they would all be reunited in the Pacific Northwest.

Early on the westward journey, on a clear summer's day, when the wagons were still following the Platte River, the Malick's seventeen-year-old son Hiram drowned. They watched him struggle in the water. It took Abigail more than a year before she could write home about his death:

> He went Aswiming with some other boys of the Compeny that we Trailed with And he swum Acrost the river and the Water run very fast And he could not reach this side. The young Men tried to save him but he [had the Cramp] And Could swim no more. And they Said o hiram do swim but he said I cannot swim eney More. And one young Man took A pole And started to him And the water ran so fast that he thought he Could not swim eney more so he returned. And left him to his fate. And the other boys Called to him and said O hiram O swim. And he said o my god I cannot eney More. They said that he went down in the water seven or eight times before he drounded. And then he said o my god O lord gesus receive My Soul for I am no More.[3]

Abigail added, "It has Almost kild Me but I have to bear it."

The Malicks registered a claim on the banks of the Columbia River, only a short distance from Fort Vancouver, which promised security against Indian uprisings. Their land seemed high enough not to be flooded, and they had more salmon that they could eat and enough lumber to sell. The Malicks were good farmers, and they worked hard. George built a porch and a milk house. On June 24, 1851, Abigail wrote, "Our house is full of good things And I have Made two new bedes cince we have bin in oregon."[4] Soon she had store-bought chairs, a bureau and mirror, and a silk dress.

The spring after they arrived, news of gold at Sutter's Mill in northern California filled the territory. George and his oldest son, Charles, joined the rush of men from every corner of the world. They brought back $5,000, more money than they had ever seen at one time. George thought that was enough, but Charles changed his clothes and went back to California. The Malicks never heard from him again. Friends said that Charles had been set upon by thieves; others said he died of brain fever. The family was never sure. Two years in Oregon Territory and the Malicks thrived, but one son was drowned and one son was missing. Around them the Willamette Valley bloomed. Oregon Territory formed its provisional government in 1843, built its trade, and moved from first settlement toward statehood.

By March 1852, the Malicks' sixteen-year-old daughter Rachel had more suitors than she could count. She chose a young lieutenant from Pennsylvania, where her parents had been raised. John Biles was a carpenter and a surveyor who wrote elegant letters. They carried on a long courtship and had an elaborate frontier wedding. Soon there was a son everybody called "Little Charlie," the beginning of new life after Hiram's death and Charles's disappearance. A year later, Rachel was pregnant again; but at her second delivery, she was carrying twins in breech position. She died screaming in pain at nineteen. John Biles fled the territory like a man pursued by demons. He gave his son to his mother-in-law and recrossed the continent, all the way back to Pennsylvania. On August 5,

1855, Abigail wrote to her daughter in Illinois, "We are All well. All that are left of us."[5]

Abigail Malick was by then a woman in her fifties, old by the standards of pioneering. She had farmed in Pennsylvania and in Illinois, and now, late in life, she came to love her claim on the Columbia River. Her daughter sent seeds from Illinois, and Abigail grew gardens that were the amazement of her neighbors. She planted orchards of apple, pear, and cherry. When her husband George died in 1853, she farmed alone, milking the cows and feeding the hogs. She hired Indians to cut the lumber and plow the fields and saw no reason to stop working. She had three younger children to raise, and she had Rachel's little boy. But raising children on the frontier was different from what it was in "the States." "They have no father," she wrote, "and they will not mind me." There was a wildness in these youngsters. Her son Shindel, nine when they came into Oregon Territory, found gambling and racing horses with the young men at Fort Vancouver more to his liking than farm work. Thirteen-year-old Jane preferred riding with handsome young officers to going to school. She was probably pregnant at fifteen, and her mother arranged a hasty marriage before a justice of the peace.

In the winter of 1855, the Rogue River Indians rose against the settlers, who scurried into Vancouver and to the fort at the Cascades. Abigail grumbled at having to leave her farm and her livestock, but her description of the Indians' resolve, written on December 8, 1855, was graphic:

> The Indians sent word that they were a coming to distroy [the] whole [of] Washington and Oregon and Burn All that the Bostons [Americans] had and Murder All And Scelpe them. So the people had All to Leave there Homes and go to the nearest towns for to protect themselves.... [Some] people ... brought in All the friendly Indians. They Were Scard As bad As the white people.... The [warring] Indians say they will fight the Americans As long as they have provisions. And [when there is nothing to eat], they will eat there Wifes And Children And fight the [Americans].[6]

By spring she wrote, "If you should not get enney Letter from us for six Months you can think that we Are All kild."[7]

By 1859, the family chaos had crossed the curve of political chaos. Jane's handsome lieutenant gambled away her dowry, and Jane came home barefoot. Abigail provided the details of the debacle:

> When They Were Maried [they] Went to the Dolls [The Dalles] to Live. And When They Went A Way He Had Nine Hundred Dollars Besides four yoke of oxen And A Nice Teem of American Horses. . . . When Jane Went A Way She Had Thousand of Cloathes And A Splended Bed. And I gave Her A First Rate cow And A Hefer Calf. . . . She Took Three Chestes Full of Cloathes And A Larg goods Box Full of Blankets and Sheates And Pillow cases And Five pares of Shooes And Stockings. . . . And When She Came Home To me she Had onley Mockones [moccasins] on Her Feet And Not Hardley Eny Cloaths. He sold Nearley [all] Her Cloathes.[8]

Jane's first child died in infancy in 1857. By the time her second child was born in 1859, she was subject to violent seizures. Her mother wrote back to Illinois on October 18, "I Have Had to Tak her Babe And Not let Her See it for two And thre days At A Time And tie her down on the Bed and it took Three of us to do it At that."[9] Abigail kept Jane's madness a family secret until December, when Jane climbed to the top of the house, stripped naked to the waist, and began to tear the shingles from the roof. Abigail sent for a soldier from Fort Vancouver, who lowered Jane to the ground with a long rope.

Eight years after her arrival in Oregon Country, Abigail Malick had an errant son, a daughter given to madness, a newborn infant, a three-year-old whose father was three thousand miles away, and a pretty fourteen-year-old who was impatient to leave home. Abigail managed the farm and tried to hold these volcanic lives together. The extended family was broken into a grand triangle. John Biles was in Pennsylvania attending seances to conjure up images of his dead wife. Mary Ann Albright and her family remained in Illinois. Abigail Malick was in Oregon on her claim on the Columbia River. It was no longer clear where the center was and, if there was one, whether it would hold. Abigail's land on the Columbia was as rich as she could want it to be, but catastrophes came close together. Without the Albrights, the Malicks were too fragile against an uncontrollable frontier, against Indians wars and childbirth, against a new idea of romance that pulled young women out of the house as surely as gold called young men. In 1860, Susan Malick eloped at sixteen. Within months, when her husband threatened to cut her throat, she divorced him, joined a troupe of traveling players and was paid twenty dollars a month—a lavish wage for a young girl in the western territories.

Mary Ann Albright urged her mother to come back to Illinois, but Abigail stayed on alone, renting half her house to strangers. She missed her grandchildren and had been a faithful correspondent for seventeen years, but she would not go back to Illinois. In 1865, when the Civil War ended, she died where she wanted to be, watching her orchards bloom on land she had cleared and cared for beside the Columbia River.

After Abigail's death, Shindel savaged his mother's claim and sold or gambled away every piece of furniture and every acre of land. He wanted no part of the legacy she had intended him to have. John Biles came back from Pennsylvania, married Elizabeth Kelly, and took little Charlie to live with him and his second wife in Portland. Susan and Shindel moved to Boise, Idaho. Abigail's letters—seventeen years of letters—found their way to a dealer who sold them for forty-five dollars to the Beinecke Library of Yale University. When I spoke with Mary Ann Albright's descendants, Abigail's great-great-grandniece, the family was still in Illinois where they had always been, but they knew nothing of the Malicks who had gone West.

Writing women's history and family history sometimes leaves a vacant canvas, the lives of ordinary people erased by adversity or mischance, the wrong key struck on the computer keyboard and the screen gone blank, the images that were once there turned into shadows that disappear. Some years ago, I visited the Vietnam Monument in Washington, D.C.

The taxi driver pointed toward the low hill faced with a long, polished, gray marble tablet. "It's over that way," he said, "but there's nothing to see." The Veterans of Foreign Wars later commissioned a traditional monument, the statue of three young soldiers carrying guns—three pioneers conquering their own wilderness.

The Vietnam Monument has a lot to do with the history of the Malicks and with the history of the Columbia River. The monument is a headstone for boys and girls remembered not because they were heroes but because we raised them and worried over them and loved them well. The wall imposes no image over our own grief. It is the same with the lives of ordinary people. Their "marker" is sometimes only their own failures and frustrations. Abigail Malick worked for her children. She sent them to school. She married them off. She gave them dowries. She would have given them her land. But the children who grew up in Oregon Territory fell too far from the tree to take root. Gnarled and indomitable, proud of having brought orchards out of the wild new land, Abigail died alone.

Some truths of American experience hover at the margins of historical imagination. C. Van Woodward said, "All history that the historian writes . . . has to be imagined before it can be written. . . . Documents and other sources help . . . but events have to be reconstructed by the imagination." Then he quoted Robert Penn Warren: "Historical sense and poetic sense should not, in the end, be contradictory, for if poetry is the little myth we make, history is the big myth we live, and in our living, constantly remake."[10] Abigail Malick is a signpost for the historian's imagination.

The Malicks, in their flamboyant failures, were far more typical of frontier life than is first apparent. For all the spectacular misadventures of their private affairs, they fall within the median range of statistics we can gather. The U.S. Census in 1850 shows forty-four families along with the Malicks in Clark County, Oregon. One decade later, only nine of those original families were still there. Eighty percent, like the Malicks, had moved on or disappeared.[11] Frontier families kept moving, and urban families did the same. According to historian Carroll Smith-

Rosenberg, the average residence in Buffalo, New York, in the 1850s was only 6.2 years. In Newburyport, Massachusetts, between 1860 and 1870, the transient rate was 65 percent.[12] John Mack Faragher found that in Illinois the persistence rate—the rate of families that stay in place—was less than 30 percent, that is, "two-thirds of heads of households moved elsewhere during the course of each decade."[13] In western cities such as San Francisco, Denver, and Omaha, at the end of the nineteenth century, the number of *different* people at any one time was five to ten times the population in place the previous decade. In Albuquerque in the 1960s and 1970s, one-sixth of the total population represented in-migration to replace one-sixth of the population that had moved out.[14] *The New York Times*, reporting on the most recent census data in 1991, noted that "nearly half of the population of the United States . . . moved from one home to another from 1985 to 1989, with about 18 percent of the nation's households pulling up stakes in 1989 alone. . . . The West . . . remained the most mobile section of the country."[15] Behind the icons of permanence—the churches and the schools and the neat tract houses—Americans keep moving on. The freedom to create new lives in some "uncreated space" is our strong need. The culture raises us to believe in our capacity and in our right to start again, and most of us believe the next time will be better.

Family, the ordered relationship of generations that touch, contradicts the need to move on. In fact, one might say family is subversive of the values Americans are taught to prize. In the moving, we are likely to leave behind parents, to leave a sister or a brother along the way. In three hundred years of following frontiers, we have learned to live with less family and to live with "family" in permutations. We have grown comfortable with family in some "dis-assembled" state. Abigail would not go back to Illinois. Her children would not live with her.

Even the bizarre details of the Malicks' story resonates in our common history. Abigail wrote of Jane's insanity as if it were an everyday event—"Since coming down from the roof, Jane has never Had Eny simptoms"—as if madness were like the common cold.[16] But there were already three asylums for the insane before 1870—in northern California, at Stockton (established in 1852), and a few years later in Oregon at Salem and Portland. The Sisters of Charity opened a House of Providence in 1856 in Vancouver to serve as both orphanage and asylum. St. Joseph's Hospital, built in 1855, did the same.[17] Reports of the insane asylum of Portland between 1870 and 1890 (deposited of all places in a dusty annex of the New York Public Library) show that the number of patients increased from 260 in 1870–1872 to 411 in 1876–1877 and to 734 in 1884–1886. Of that number, the fraction of female patients started at one-third and grew to one-half.[18]

But the numbers need to be transformed into images—Jane Malick as a young bride coming home barefoot from The Dalles, dancing half naked on the roof of her mother's house, pulling off the shingles, carried down by an embarrassed young soldier assigned a task he had never contemplated. I think of Jane tied to her bed so that she could not harm her own baby. She was barely more than a child herself, thrust into a turbulent land, like Herman Melville's black cabin boy Pip, frightened into madness by the ferocity of the quest for Moby Dick. I think of Jane as a sister to Benjy, the idiot and loving heart of Faulkner's *The Sound and the Fury*. Jane was not a heroic bronze tribute to the pioneer mother, but she managed to outlive her madness. She remarried, had children, and in later life tried to temper the passions of her irritable sister and brother. If not exactly whole, Jane was a serviceable frontier woman. I think of nineteen-year-old Rachel who died in childbirth after the doctor botched the delivery of twins, trying to dismember the infants so he could get them out of their mother's womb. That is also a frontier story.

Most of all, I think of Abigail, who came into Oregon and built a home for her wayward children, who grew orchards out of the wilderness. On September 9, 1861, Abigail wrote:

> We will Have An Abundance of chois Fruit. Pears And Apples And plums And Siberian Crab[apples] And peaches and Cheryes of difent kindes and Chois Apples Sutch As I Never Saw Eny In the states. I paid thirty Dollars For My Fruit trees and Currentes. There Will Be No End to them And goosburyes And Tame Ras-

buryes. I have Five difrent plum trees. . . . And four pare trees And
I do not know how Meny peach trees And rasing More All the time.
And I do not know how Meny Apple trees.[19]

Abigail's fruit trees were her true children. But the frontier images soon
disappear. Stephen Dow Beckham checked the old survey maps of Vancouver for me and found that the Malicks' claim became industrial land
with grain-loading facilities on the riverbank.

America's westward course has created different frontiers, born of geography and of the mind. Thomas Jefferson imagined a frontier of yeo-
man farmers, where men and earth were bound to each other in the
benediction of fruitful labor. Jefferson's image of the Garden holds family and land in balance. It is what the poet Wendell Berry called "the gift
of good land," a vision that resonates through our history.[20] It is a dream
of order and Christian blessing and the continuity of generations, peace
on a bountiful land. Abigail's orchards were proof of the goodness of the
land and of the efficacy of work.

The Malick children preferred a different frontier. They preferred the
spectacle and the promises of gold and silver in California and Idaho.
The frontier they chose was a place of high stakes and low jokes, a place
for buffoonery and swagger, where Shindel could race horses and
gamble, where Susan could join a group of traveling players, and where
Jane married a man her mother considered shiftless, "mean," and
"dirty." Mining and gambling frontiers were the landscape of tricksters
and wizards, sleight-of-hand merchants performing behind the sur-
veyors' offices, singing at the door of the land agent. And even though
Abigail's children might be hungry or barefoot, they did not want to stay
home. There were frontiers of such hardship that grown men cried, because they could not erase memories of living in a "coyote hole," or of
children indentured to strangers because they could not be fed. Frontiers
frame conflicting images and bid newcomers test which one would hold
their future.

Bart Giamatti, when he was president of Yale University, wrote about
baseball because he saw it as a peculiarly American game, a ritualized

performance about the skill and crazy daring one needed to reach the "frontiers"—first base, second base, third—and then to endure the anguish and the perils of finally reaching "home."

> When a player rounds third, a long journey seemingly over, the end in sight, then the hunger for home, the drive to rejoin one's earlier self and one's fellows, is a pressing, growing, screaming in the blood. Often the effort fails, the hunger is unsatisfied as the catcher bars fulfillment, as the umpire-father is too strong in his denial, as the impossibility of going home again is re-enacted in what is often baseball's most violent confrontations, swift, savage, down in the dirt, availing nothing. If baseball is a narrative, an epic of exile and return, a vast communal poem about separation, loss and home for a reunion—. . . It is the romance of homecoming that America sings to itself.[21]

Home and the ways we leave it, frontiers and what they bring us—these are the thoughts I have wanted to share. The Malicks are what novelist Toni Morrison called "the deep story," the "coded language" of the American experience, the story of what frontiers have meant to families.[22] Beyond the Malicks, family and frontiers are the coordinates of an ongoing American debate, the magnets of our minds, a morality so cleverly charged that the polar points force each other apart. However we may yearn to come within the circle of home, we are also absolutely determined to escape its boundaries. American frontiers leave a complex emotional legacy, but so does family. Gathered around the Thanksgiving table, family is caught for a moment in the Instamatic camera. Then it breaks apart, not family at all, but the "frontiers" of private and separate lives.

The Malicks' story is a meditation on the American self. Perhaps in the end, they endure in their letters, with their flashbacks, omissions, and the ways in which they skewed the truth. The letters somehow join our lives and theirs. We know the Malicks very well. We know them better, perhaps, than they ever knew each other.

NOTES

1. Lillian Schlissel, *Women's Diaries of the Westward Journey* (New York: Schocken Books, 1982).

2. Schlissel et al., *Far from Home: Families of the Westward Journey* (New York: Schocken Books, 1989).

3. Ibid., 10.

4. Ibid., 14.

5. Ibid., 45.

6. Ibid., 50.

7. Ibid., 51.

8. Ibid., 70.

9. Ibid., 75.

10. C. Van Woodward, *The Future of the Past* (New York: Oxford University Press, 1989), 233–4.

11. *Federal Population Census for Oregon Territory, 1850–1960* (Washington, D.C.: National Archive Trust Fund Board, 1979).

12. Carroll Smith-Rosenberg, "Bourgeois Discourse and the Progressive Era," in *Disorderly Conduct: Visions of Gender in Victorian America* (New York: A. A. Knopf, 1985), 169.

13. John Mack Faragher, *Sugar Creek: Life on the Illinois Prairie* (New Haven: Yale University Press, 1986), 50.

14. Peter A. Morrison and Judith P. Wheeler, "The Image of 'Elsewhere' in the American Tradition of Migration" (paper presented at a symposium on Human Migration, American Academy of Arts and Sciences, New Harmony, Indiana, April 1976) 4. See also George W. Pierson, "The M Factor in American History," in Michael McGiffert, ed., *The Character of Americans: A Book of Readings*, rev. ed. (Homewood, Ill.: Dorsey Press, 1970), 118–30.

15. *The New York Times*, December 29, 1991.

16. Schlissel et al., *Far from Home*, 78.

17. Lee Stolmack, "Care and Treatment of the Mentally Disordered in California, 1849–1862" (Honors project, Department of History, California State University, Sacramento, 1979); Fred Lockley, "The Story of Vancouver," *Oregon Journal* (May 18, 1930): 4.

18. Oregon Insane Asylum, Portland, Oregon, *Reports of Physicians* (papers in New York Public Library, 1870–72, 1876–78, 1884–96). See also Richard Fox, *So Far Disordered in Mind: Insanity in California, 1870–1930* (Berkeley: University of California Press, 1979).

19. Schlissel et al., *Far from Home*, 92.

20. Wendell Berry, *The Gift of Good Land: Further Essays, Cultural and Agricultural* (San Francisco: North Point Press, 1981).

21. A. Bartlett Giamatti, "The Story of Baseball: You Can Go Home Again," from "Americans and Their Games," *The New York Times*, April 2, 1989.

22. Toni Morrison, *Playing in the Dark: Whiteness and the Literary Imagination* (Cambridge, Mass.: Harvard University Press, 1992), 6.

Changing Cultural Inventions
of the Columbia

BY RICHARD W. ETULAIN

*A*llow me to begin with what anthropologists call ethnographic evidence—what we historians call an anecdote—in this case, a family story.

Just as I had puberty in sight, the Etulains moved from Ritzville to Ellensburg, Washington. The move was more than just crossing the Columbia, more than a jaunt of 150 miles. We were abandoning a 10,000-acre stock ranch twenty-two miles from the nearest town, surrounded by fertile wheat ranches, and moving to a 300-acre farm in the Kittitas Valley, known for its cattle and hay ranches and small, irrigated farms. If Ritzville orbited around Spokane on the outer edges of the Inland Empire, Ellensburg wavered under the hegemony of Seattle and the coast. Before my senior year, we recrossed the Columbia—again at Vantage—to relocate in Moses Lake, the center of the Columbia Basin. Now off the ranch and farm, we ended up in a town, squeezed between a mushrooming irrigation empire and a sprawling military domain.

What the Etulains lived through in these three locations, many northwesterners have experienced during the last century: the Columbia River as both a powerful unifying and a dividing force. On many occasions, residents have represented the Columbian empire as an identifiable region, separate from surrounding areas. In other situations, northwesterners in eastern Washington and Oregon, Idaho, and western Montana have asserted they are another part of the Northwest, isolated and different from the coastal trough stretching from the Canadian to California borders.

The experiences of the Etulain family epitomize still another set of shifting images of the Pacific Northwest. When my Basque sheepherding father settled in eastern Washington, he carved out a ranch previously without buildings, fences, or roads. He thought of himself as both immigrant and frontiersman. But less than two generations later we were surrounded by huge symbols of American agribusiness and military might. We had obviously moved past frontier and beyond nascent region and were catapulted into something of a postregion. Many northwesterners have experienced similar sharp shifts during the last century, and their descriptions of these transformations are often intriguing searches for self-identification. The writings of novelists and historians are particularly useful barometers of these traumatic cultural changes.

In the century following Captain Robert Gray's entrance into the Columbia in 1792, explorers, travelers, overlanders, settlers, and a wide assortment of observers depicted the river and its inland empire in rich and varied hues. Some viewed it as a giant window on the Pacific, others as a necessary link with China and Indian trade, and still others as a frontier to be conquered, civilized, and exploited. Lewis and Clark, Astor's men, Oregon Trail pioneers, early entrepreneurs, and even the first novelists and historians echoed these outward-looking and inward-turning interpretations of the Columbian province as an open frontier whose native peoples and varied landscapes should be won over and utilized. These viewpoints persisted throughout the nineteenth century and into at least two or three decades of the twentieth.

The vision of the Pacific Northwest as an area ripe for civilizing is at the center of Frederic Homer Balch's *Bridge of the Gods* (1890), the most popular Northwest novel of its time and continuously in print for more than a century. Drawing on his own experiences living on both sides of the Columbia (near Lyle on the north and Hood River on the south), his readings in nearly all major nineteenth-century historical works about the Oregon Country, and his interviews with Indians and early settlers, Balch fashioned a highly romantic, sentimental, and improbable novel about a newly arrived missionary's contact with a sprawling Indian confederacy in the late eighteenth century. But the limitations of *Bridge of the Gods*, large and numerous though they be, are less significant here than Balch's treatment of the symbolic import of the Columbia River and its immediate surroundings.

The riverine system that Balch depicts unites as well as divides its cultural hinterlands. In the novel, Native American tribes from the upper reaches of the Columbia in the Okanogan country, southward nearly one thousand miles to the headwaters of the Willamette, and east to the backcountry of the Snake are inexorably drawn to the Indian confederacy centered near the confluence of the Columbia and the Willamette. Here the mighty Willamette chieftain Multnomah vaunts his power that reaches out, like tentacles, into the far corners of the Pacific Northwest. Yet, these far-flung tribes also reveal their differences and divisions. Angry chieftains and rebellious bands, especially those in eastern Oregon and Washington and along the Snake, fiercely challenge much of Multnomah's hegemony.

Fittingly, near the end of the novel, when rancor, competition, and belligerence destroy the shaky confederacy, a powerful earthquake erupts, demolishing the giant natural bridge spanning the Columbia. The collapse of the "bridge of the gods," along with the death of Multnomah, signals the breakup of Indian alliances. These linkages destroyed, the native peoples retreat to their fragmented, deadly competition. Only the Columbia remains. As Balch intones in the final paragraphs of his novel:

> Blue and majestic in the sunlight flows the Columbia, river of many names . . . always vast and grand, always flowing placidly to the sea. . . . Generation after generation . . . all the shadowy peoples of the past have sailed its waters . . . and still the river holds its course, bright, beautiful, inscrutable. It stays; *we go*.[1]

Not all novelists or visitors of Balch's era saw the Columbia as he did, however.

Some travelers to the Pacific Northwest at the end of the century also commented on the significance of the Columbia to the region. In the decade before the publication of his best-selling novel *The Virginian* (1902), Owen Wister, snobbish Philadelphian with newly acquired Harvard airs, traveled to central Washington, first to gather materials for his fiction and then for his honeymoon. Forced to stay a weekend in Coulee City, Wister condemns the hamlet from end to end. It is, he writes, "a sordid community . . . huddled there in the midst of unlimited nothing." Coulee, he adds,

> is too dead even for much crime. . . . Nobody got either drunk or dangerous. People have been killed there, I believe, but not too often, most likely not lately. There is but one professional woman in the whole town, and from what I heard the men say, she is a forlorn old wreck, so unsightly that even her monopoly brings no profit.[2]

Most of the terrain Wister encounters east of the Columbia he dismisses as barren, ugly, useless stretches of sage and waste. He is more attracted to the wooded areas west of the river, finding in them less uncivilized western life to denounce.

During their honeymoon in 1898, Wister and his new bride were repulsed by the areas surrounding the Columbia in central Washington. In nearby Winthrop, Molly Wister encounters "miles and miles of what seemed like the most unlovely wilderness, almost desolation. . . . Everything seemed stern and unforgiving. You can hardly imagine what the impression of nature with its beauty and tenderness left out is like." She had to admit, however, that the isolation and repose gradually grew on her, acknowledging, finally, that she could "be happy here for a long time." Her husband was less reconciled, declaring the Columbia "the most dreadful thing I have ever seen. . . . It is something to have nightmares about for 20 years. . . . It lies in a rut [and the surrounding hills] make a vast endless winding cleft of prison."[3]

Englishman Rudyard Kipling, arriving in the Pacific Northwest by way of India a few years before Wister, also displayed ambivalent reactions to the Columbia and its environs. Dismissing Portland as too busy with boosterism, building, and violence to pave its streets and manage its sewage, Kipling fled up the Willamette and Columbia rivers as far as The Dalles. The wooded shores and other green scenes—especially Bridal Veil Falls—are immensely attractive to him; and so are the running schools of salmon, although Kipling's graphic account of their being netted, filleted, and stuffed into cans suggests his revulsion at technology's destruction of nature. Meanwhile, The Dalles, called tongue-in-cheek "the center of a great sheep and wool district, and the head of navigation," is described as without "peace and purity," an uncivilized blemish on the Great River of the West.

Later, after a return to Portland and a quick visit to booming Tacoma, Washington, Kipling's party travels through verdant forests, only to emerge into a "wilderness of sage brush" near the Columbia. Yet, Kipling added, "one thing worse than sage unadulterated . . . is a prairie city. We stopped at Pasco Junction, and a man told me that it was the Queen City of the Prairie. I wish Americans didn't tell such useless lies."[4] Once the Englishman and his companions dashed through eastern Washington and re-entered the forested Rockies, his spirits revived.

Historians writing about a late-nineteenth-century Pacific Northwest were less inclined to see the dreary, uncivilized scenes and residents that vividly colored the reactions of Wister and Kipling. Between the 1880s and the 1920s, several historians produced pioneer accounts of the Pacific Northwest, with stress on the Columbia River, but their emphases were more prosaic than those in contemporary novels and travel accounts.

In the most extensive historical accounts published in the second half of the nineteenth century, H. H. Bancroft—better yet, Frances Fuller Victor, since she wrote most of the volumes—established a framework and periodization that historians seemed to follow for several decades. In two volumes on the Northwest coast (1883, 1886) and in other thick tomes on Oregon, Washington, Idaho, Montana, and British Columbia,

Bancroft-Victor details the numerous explorers who traversed the coast and inlets looking for passages into the interior. Then follow long chapters on subsequent overland explorations, fur trade competitions, diplomatic controversies, and first settlements. In all these discussions, the Columbia River plays conspicuous roles as a mysterious site, an avenue of eastern- and westward-moving exploration, an area of geographical/diplomatic competition, and a location of pioneer settlements. Overall, the Columbia country becomes a frontier, where newcomers confront novel terrain and new peoples and where they deal with challenging wilderness settings. None of these extensive volumes follows the story long enough or with sufficient insight to see beyond the Columbia as new frontier. Another half-century or more had to elapse before historians would begin to ask about the centripetal and centrifugal influences of the Columbia River.[5]

A generation later, long-time Oregon historian Joseph Schafer situated the Columbia on center stage in much of his story of the early Pacific Northwest. The prime importance of the river to exploration, the fur trade, and diplomatic negotiations is repeatedly emphasized in Schafer's *History of the Pacific Northwest* (1905). Once he treats these earliest contacts and conflicts, however, Schafer abandons the Columbia except to note it as dividing the new state of Oregon and Washington Territory and as the best route to the interior Northwest. But even these treatments are brief and fleeting. Schafer seems unaware of the Columbia as a backbone of a regional trade or transportational grid. Indeed, like nearly all historians of his time, he views the Columbia as a frontier rather than as a regional symbol.

The following year, the immensely influential Frederick Jackson Turner published his only completed monograph, *Rise of the New West, 1819–1829*, which, its title notwithstanding, devotes but one of nineteen chapters to the Far West. Although Turner only glancingly mentions the Columbia or the Pacific Northwest, he did see the river system as both a unifying and a dividing force. "The two great branches of the Columbia," he pointed out, "the one reaching up into Canada, and the other pushing far into the Rocky Mountains, on the American side, constituted lines of advance for the rival forces of England and the United States in the struggle for the Oregon country." And, a half-century before Henry Nash Smith's striking elucidation of the West as a Passage to India, Turner highlights the pregnant significance of Senator Thomas Hart Benton's dreamy prediction that "the valley of the Columbia might become the granary of China and Japan, and an outlet to their imprisoned and exuberant population."[6] As he did elsewhere, Turner agrees with those who viewed the American frontier and the West as a safety valve for needy and restless immigrants. But a new perspective about the Columbia and the Pacific Northwest was just over the horizon.

The regionalist movement that spouted in the Pacific Northwest during the 1920s was but one current of a nationwide flood that poured over all regions of the country. During the decade after World War I, journalists, historians, novelists, and painters, among others, turned cheerleaders for bold, new investigations of American regions and their cultures. In New England, the South, the Midwest, and the Far West, editors of dozens of regional magazines often led the charge, sometimes echoing the cries of other Pied Pipers for less addiction to alien cultural institutions and more scrutiny and celebration of local history and society. Participating in this cultural transition, writers and artists of the Pacific Northwest who focused on the Columbia in their works avoided viewing it solely as a frontier expanding into new lands and confronting new peoples. More often, they saw the Columbia as defining a region (or subregion), gradually spawning its own cultural identity. Still, the regional perspective did not entirely supplant the frontier viewpoint; instead, it arose as an alternative, competing vista gaining in popularity during the next generation.[7]

A number of notable transformations helped to usher in this rising regionalism. World War I, the social and cultural disruptions of the 1920s, the heightened migration west, especially to areas like Los Angeles, served to draw attention to the American West. At the same time, ironically, the peaking popularity of writers like Zane Grey, Max Brand, and Clarence Mulford, of an artist such as Charlie Russell, and of hundreds of western films kept things western in front of millions of Americans. It also kept them attentive to other cultural depictions of the West, even if those treatments dealt with a regional rather than a frontier West. Furthermore, the same spirit that fostered greater interest in things regional in the South—particularly among novelists, poets, and historians—also helped ignite a regional revival in the West and in other regions as well. Even though literary and cultural historians often refer to the 1920s and 1930s as the era of the Lost Generation, the Roaring Twenties, the Great Depression, the New Deal, and the proletarian era, it was likewise a generation of regionalism, with writers, painters, photographers, and planners discovering or rediscovering pulsating regional cultures throughout every part of the United States.

No writer more than H. L. Davis illustrates the surge of regionalism that washed over the Pacific Northwest during the 1920s and 1930s. The product of a peripatetic family that hopscotched throughout central and eastern Oregon early in the twentieth century, Davis naturally drew on these scenes and experiences for a series of lively sketches, stories, and novels published between the late 1920s and 1960. A skilled raconteur and committed regionalist, Davis always had difficulty keeping his picaresque characters together and headed in the same direction. Alongside his dozens of vignettes depicting coastal hamlets, ranching and farming settlements, and wandering workers are numerous descriptions of the Columbia, the travelers on it, and the river towns perched on its banks. Almost all of these works treat a postfrontier Northwest, a generation or two beyond initial white settlements. Moreover, well acquainted with the western and Mississippi writings of Mark Twain and buoyed by the encouragement of cultural pundit H. L. Mencken, Davis suffused his prose with a humor, iconoclasm, and satire reminiscent of those two writers.

One of the earliest of the sketches, "A Town in Eastern Oregon," illustrates the witty and sardonic tone that characterizes most of Davis's writings dealing with the Columbia. A rambling, abbreviated history of Gros Ventre (no doubt "gross venture"), it is a thinly disguised satire of The Dalles. The town was settled by backtrailers, Davis recounts, who wanted to settle in western Oregon but who found those areas too crowded and thus, reluctantly, backslid to eastern Oregon. Once there, this backwash of the pioneer movement, especially in river towns like Gros Ventre, was not solid citizens of pioneer heroic tradition but primarily wanderers lusting after quick riches. "The amount of devilment and cussedness that its citizens have succeeded in whipping out of its corporate limits since it was founded," quips Davis, "would line Hell a hundred miles."[8] Over time, missionaries, soldiers, and merchants—and later steamboatmen, railroaders, and freighters—invaded the town and attempted to civilize it by driving off all undesirables in the name of Civic Improvement. Those unable or unwilling to submit to the puritanical demands of the city fathers were thrown out.

Five years later in his first and Pulitzer Prize–winning novel *Honey in the Horn*, Davis interjected another section on The Dalles among descriptions of several other subregions of Oregon. The hero encounters a windy steamboat captain who puts him to work steering and looking after his boat. On the river, everything seems Edenic, quiet, peaceful, and safe. But once ashore in a variety of two-bit hellholes, brimming with thieves, prostitutes, drunks, and those who wish they were so, he discovers life at its lowest ebb, muddied with the foulest and greediest of human animals. The distance between the pacific river and clanging, amoral riverbank towns reminds one of Twain's moral geography: the big dark brown "God" of the Mississippi and the "barbaric yawp" of the phony and defiled citizens of the river towns. Like Twain, Davis seemed convinced of the rectitude of the peaceful river and the irredeemable decay and violence of society hunkered down on its banks.

Davis's treatment of the Columbia and river towns is but chapter-length in "A Town in Eastern Oregon" and in *Honey in the Horn*, but that emphasis moves to center stage and occupies the whole of his later novel *The Distant Music* (1957). This story describes a three-generation family, the Mulocks, putting down roots in the Columbia River town of Clark's Landing (The Dalles area, where Davis resided for nearly two decades). The three Ranse Mulocks—grandfather, son, and grandson—fight off their pasts, attempt to learn from one another, and display tormented, love/hate attitudes toward the Landing. The power of the riverside land holds them, in spite of their longings to flee from it. Most of the novel's central metaphors—including the pull of epiphanic "distant music," its major protagonists, and the book's plot—are linked to an interplay between setting and characters. Here is the central theme of the regionalist: how, over time, place has shaped the lives of residents. Along the shores of the Columbia, gradually, a regional identity results when several generations react to the land, to one another, and to the legacies of history bequeathed to them. In the closing chapters of this racy, vernacular novel, one of the central characters, *griot*-like, recaps the history of the Landing, squeezing the past for its secrets, empathetically scrutinizing the journeys of the town's residents, and concluding how the passage of time has laminated these experiences into a recognizable regional society and culture.

The regional bug bit other Northwest novelists besides H. L. Davis, but most did not focus on the Columbia. Davis's best friend, James Stevens, depicted life in the woods and among radical laborers; and Mormon novelist Vardis Fisher was even more voluminous, writing more than a dozen historical novels about southeastern Idaho and American pioneers of the nineteenth century and a string of novels treating human history from prehistoric to near-present times. Nard Jones and Archie Binns turned out several historical and romance novels, all competently done and some treating the Columbia River, included Jones's *Swift Flows the River* (1940), *Scarlet Petticoat* (1941), and *Still to the West* (1946) and Binns's *Lightship* (1934) and *Yon Rolling River* (1947). None of these novels approaches the high level of Davis's best regional fiction, although the latest of Jones's novels contains a good deal of interesting commentary on the building of Grand Coulee Dam.

Historians and painters in the Pacific Northwest were slower than novelists of the region and historians and novelists of other parts of the West to treat the Northwest regionally. Although Walter Prescott Webb and James Malin published regional histories of the Great Plains and Kansas during the 1930s and 1940s and artists Thomas Hart Benton,

Grant Wood, and John Steuart Curry completed widely publicized regionalist paintings during the same period, historians and painters of the
Northwest were less forward-looking.

Still, historians betrayed some interest in examining the Pacific
Northwest as a developing region. In the most widely used general history of the region in the 1930s and early 1940s, *A History of the Pacific
Northwest* (1931), George W. Fuller supplied prefatory chapters on the
settings and natives of the region before launching into standard sections
on explorations, fur traders, missionaries, and settlers, with a final chapter tiptoeing into the twentieth century. The Columbia receives little unusual attention, except for a glancing discussion of a projected Grand
Coulee Dam and Columbia Basin Project. A decade and a half later, the
first edition of Oscar Osborn Winther's *The Great Northwest: A History*
(1947) appeared, with the author's pronouncement that the region had
"come of age. Long an important hinterland, it [had] finally emerged as
one of the very significant sections of the nation."[9] How that specific regional identity had evolved, however, was not an explicit theme in
Winther's text. Indeed, only in devoting 70 of 350 pages to the post-1900
era did Winther break noticeably from previous historical overviews.
Briefly discussing the Columbia's role in early diplomacy and transportation, the author celebrated Grand Coulee Dam as the "Eighth Wonder of the World" and mentioned the river's recent significance as a
source of irrigation waters and hydroelectric power.

Nearly twice as long as Winther's account, *Empire of the Columbia:
A History of the Pacific Northwest* (1957), by Dorothy O. Johansen and
Charles M. Gates, now in its second edition, remains the most extensive
history of the region. Expanding on the Columbia's central role in the
earliest explorations and in later diplomatic and transportation efforts,
the authors demonstrated, more than previous scholars, the river's important agency in the development of fisheries, shipping, and irrigation. Furthermore, Professor Gates was the first to show how the region
rapidly became an urban-dominated area between 1880 and 1910, its
largest populations and economic strength moving away from a river
hegemony toward that of cities. *Empire on the Columbia* was, and re-

mains, a pathbreaking work of regional history; for the first time, readers were treated to a full history of the Pacific Northwest from its earliest frontiers through its establishment of a new regional identity.

World War II transformed the American West as no other previous event, except perhaps the Gold Rush, had done. Slashing across the Pacific Northwest, the war years revolutionized the economy of the region, as they did those of other subregions of the West, particularly those sectors involved in military-industrial developments. The events of those years also dramatically altered the region's sociocultural configuration and redefined its linkages with the nation and the globe. Not surprisingly, these striking changes, and those erupting a generation later during the 1960s, forced novelists and historians to re-imagine the Pacific Northwest and to describe the Columbia River and its influences in pathbreaking terms. Overall, a new postregional spirit emerged and with it more complex ways to describe the Pacific Northwest.

Postregional culture in the Pacific Northwest not only included earlier frontier and regional visions of the Far Corners but it also incorporated revised perspectives on older topics and encompassed new subjects. Postregionalism was thus inclusive rather than exclusive, illustrating the increasing complexity rather than the simplicity of the region and its cultures. Fittingly, the most recent interpretations of the Great River of the West illustrate this growing intricacy.

Several novelists whose careers began as early as the 1920s continued to publish novels with frontier or regional perspectives well past World War II. For example, three novels by Ernest Haycox—*Long Storm* (1946), *The Earthbreakers* (1952), and *The Adventurers* (1955)—focus on pioneer Oregon and include appealing depictions of the Columbia and its tributaries as notable transportation avenues in the development of the frontier Northwest. In the generation following 1945, A. B. Guthrie, Jr. (*The Way West*, 1949), Dorothy Johnson (*Indian Country*, 1953), and Vardis Fisher (*Tale of Valor*, 1958; *Mountain Man*, 1965) also published historical fiction treating the frontier or regional Pacific Northwest.

Gradually, however, new emphases helped to redefine the Northwest past and present. Novelists such as Ivan Doig and other members of the

Montana "school" stressed subregional experiences without falling victim to a numbing provincialism. As early as the 1930s, in D'Arcy McNickle's fiction and later in the writings of James Welch, Janet Campbell Hale, and Sherman Alexie, Native Americans accented ethnicity as much, or even more, as place in redefining the Northwest. Sophus K. Winther, John Okada, Craig Lesley, and David Guterson also called attention to immigrant or ethnic groups as important actors in the history of the Pacific Northwest. For Janet Campbell Hale and Marilynne Robinson, matters of gender and family merited more attention than the shaping power of geography. At the same time, a more pronounced environmental perspective colors the works of several writers. For example, A. B. Guthrie, Jr., implied that mountain men, overlanders, ranchers, and townspeople overlooked or discounted the ecological impact of their errands into the West. More recently, Ernest Callenbach, in his novel/position paper *Ecotopia* (1977), and Ivan Doig, in his autobiography and in his several Montana novels, make readers much more aware of people-land relationships than had earlier novelists.

Nor should one overlook the counter-classics or anti-Westerns of several recent writers. Ken Kesey uses Northwest settings to deal with conflicts between frustrated individualists and a suffocating, centralizing bureaucracy in his *One Flew over the Cuckoo's Nest* (1962) and *Sometimes a Great Notion* (1964). Both volumes, as well as other novels by Tom Robbins, Richard Brautigan, and David Wagoner, employ humor, irony, and satire to parody stylized heroes and villains appearing in popular Western films and fiction. These revisionist novels are clearly remythologizing the American West. Ethnic heroes, lively heroines, and new antiheroes have shot the Virginians, the Lassiters, and the John Waynes out of their saddles.

Although historians treating the Northwest since the 1960s are moving in similar postregional directions, journalists and historians such as Stewart Holbrook, David Lavender, and Nancy Wilson Ross preferred, in anecdotal narratives, to deal with the Pacific Northwest as a persisting frontier or a newly developed region. Other writers wished to discuss whether the area was, in fact, a separate region. One of the most provocative of these discussions was the Writers' Conference on the Northwest held in Portland in the fall of 1946. Reflecting a variety of interpretations and often contradictory opinions about the Northwest, more than a dozen authors addressed the central question of whether the Pacific Northwest was a separate identifiable region in *Northwest Harvest: A Regional Stock-Taking* (1948). Distinguished critic Carl Van Doren was convinced that the Northwest merited identification as a region, whereas popular novelist Ernest Haycox did not think so. Other contributors, including professors H. G. Merriam and Joseph Harrison and journalist Joseph Kinsey Howard, urged northwesterners to study their recent culture and to take stock of varying districts within the Northwest.[10]

These two final urgings have been heeded recently, with scholars now paying added attention to the twentieth century and to subregions of the Northwest. As a pioneer in these areas, Earl Pomeroy demonstrates in his analytical essays and books the importance of scrutinizing the recent past as well as examining eastern influences on the Far West. Geographer Donald W. Meinig, in *The Great Columbia Plain*, surely one of the most significant books about a western subregion, illustrates how a careful study in historical geography can illuminate people-environment relationships. In more abbreviated fashion, historians David Stratton and Judith Austin also urge readers to pay more attention to the East-West, interior-coastal divisions of the Pacific Northwest.[11]

Revisions of earlier regional overviews and new syntheses of the Northwest also reveal how much postregional emphases are evident in recent historiography. The second edition of *Empire of the Columbia* expands its discussions of the modern region and adds coverage of ethnic groups. Meanwhile, Gordon Dodds's textbook, treating Washington and Oregon (but not Idaho) and reflecting recent historiographical shifts, includes generous sections on ethnic groups, women, and other sociocultural topics. These emphases are even more pronounced in Carlos A. Schwantes, *The Pacific Northwest: An Interpretive History* (1996), a narrative loaded with vignettes of multi-ethnic peoples, discussions of gender, and particularly thorough treatments of environmental topics, the twentieth century, and the major subregions of the area.

But have these historiographical shifts influenced the ways we look at the Columbia? Do these transitions from frontier to regional to postregional emphases transform our images of the Great River of the West? They obviously do, in several explicit ways. Race, gender, and environment have clearly shoved aside frontier and region as the newest topics of widespread interest; in the last generation, contacts with new lands and new peoples and a developing regional consciousness have fallen before New Social and New Western histories.

Now, we have re-invented the Columbia River. Recent novelists and historians are more intrigued with questions about Indian fishing rights, the appropriateness of dams, giant reclamation projects, and, perhaps, Rivers of Empire. The specter of Hanford, little mentioned before the 1960s, has now become a controversial, much-discussed subject. Revealingly, Richard White, in his masterful overview of the West, speaks little of the nineteenth- or early twentieth-century roles of the Columbia but includes this attention-catching paragraph ringing with postregional emphasis:

> Marvels, however, come at a cost. Bonneville, Grand Coulee, and their numerous smaller successors reduced the Columbia, which Americans had long celebrated as symbol of the nation and the West, to a series of lakes. The Columbia no longer ran mightily to the sea; instead, the river ran between its dams like a circus lion jumping through hoops. On the Columbia above the Grand Coulee Dam, where spawning salmon had once run in the millions, the salmon ran no more. The engineers who designed the dam had given no thought to the migration of salmon up the river, and the fish vanished from the upper Columbia.[12]

At the same time, the index of Patricia Nelson Limerick's *Legacy of Conquest*, the most widely cited of the New Western histories, contains no entry for the Columbia, but her lively book does include engaging discussions of much-needed Indian fishing rights and the dangers of Hanford.

Enough periodizing and example giving. A final larger question suggests itself: do these shifting emphases among novelists and historians furnish any guidance on better ways to understand the past and our interpretations of it? I think so.

Nearly fifty years ago in his pathbreaking book *Virgin Land: The American West as Symbol and Myth* (1950), Henry Nash Smith explained how Frederick Jackson Turner and his frontier thesis were embedded in mythic notions about the West during the nineteenth century. "Whatever the merits or demerits of the frontier hypothesis in explaining actual events," Smith concluded, "the hypothesis itself developed out of the myth of the garden." Smith then proceeded to show how much Turner reflected popular notions concerning the shaping influences of nature/civilization and agriculture on American and European thinkers of the nineteenth century.[13]

Are similar insights to be derived from the shifting interpretations of the Columbia during the last century? Clearly, those depicting the river in the early twentieth century saw it as part of a frontier to be conquered; later regionalists viewed it as part of a region's progress and development; and more recently, still others, reflecting postregional attitudes, emphasize other topics. Shouldn't these changing interpretations, arising out of changing sociocultural conditions, remind us of what Smith concluded about Frederick Jackson Turner? Put another way, isn't the most probing historiography oxymoronic—not mine, not yours, but *ours*? Conversely, isn't the most dangerous trend toward hydroponic historiography, one fertilized by the conviction that only the present generation has unlocked the secrets of the past and one nourished by a destructive individualism, dismissing earlier views to champion a newer one?

So, shouldn't we conclude that all frontier, regional, and postregional perspectives supply useful interpretations of the Great River of the West? Moreover, hasn't the Columbia *both* unified and divided the Pacific Northwest? Obviously, yes, to both questions. When these acts of mental synthesis occur, our views of the Columbia, like our conclusions about the western past, become more complex, cumulative, and ever-changing. When we glimpse this longer, larger vision, we shall be freed from an Ahabian hubris and see the elephant of the greater river of the West.

NOTES

1. Frederic Homer Balch, *Bridge of the Gods* (Chicago: A. C. McClurg, 1890), 279, 280.

2. Fanny Kemble Wister, ed., *Owen Wister Out West: His Journals and Letters* (Chicago: University of Chicago Press, 1958), 136.

3. Quoted in Ben Merchant Vorpahl, *My Dear Wister: The Frederic Remington–Owen Wister Letters* (Palo Alto, Calif.: American West Publishing Company, 1972), 236, 234–35. For full descriptions of Wister's reactions to the Columbia area, see the helpful narrative in Darwin Payne, *Owen Wister: Chronicler of the West, Gentleman of the East* (Dallas: Southern Methodist University Press, 1985).

4. Arrell Morgan Gibson, ed., *American Notes: Rudyard Kipling's West* (Norman: University of Oklahoma Press, 1981), 56, 57, 77.

5. William L. Lang has published a very useful overview of these early historical treatments of the Columbia. Consult his "Creating the Columbia: Historians and the Great River of the West, 1930–1935," *Oregon Historical Quarterly* 93 (Fall 1992): 235–61.

6. Frederick Jackson Turner, *Rise of the New West, 1819–1829* (New York: Harper and Brothers, 1906), 117, 132.

7. Especially helpful for understanding the rise of regionalism in the West and South is Robert L. Dorman, *Revolt of the Provinces: The Regionalist Movement in America, 1920–1945* (Chapel Hill: University of North Carolina Press, 1993).

8. H. L. Davis, "A Town in Eastern Oregon," in *Team Bells Woke Me and Other Stories* (New York: William Morrow and Company, 1953), 175. The story originally appeared in *American Mercury Magazine* in January 1930.

9. Oscar Osborn Winther, *The Great Northwest: A History* (New York: Alfred A. Knopf, 1947), vii.

10. Carl Van Doren, "One Nation, Not Indivisible"; Ernest Haycox, "Is There a Northwest?"; Harold G. Merriam, "Does the Northwest Believe in Itself?"; Joseph B. Harrison, "Regionalism Is Not Enough"; Joseph Kinsey Howard, "Culture, Climate, and Community," in V. L. O. Chittick, ed., *Northwest Harvest: A Regional Stock-Taking* (New York: Macmillan Company, 1948).

11. Earl Pomeroy, "Toward a Reorientation of Western History: Continuity and Environment," *Mississippi Valley Historical Review* 41 (March 1955): 579–

600, and *The Pacific Slope: A History of California, Oregon, Washington, Idaho, Utah, and Nevada* (New York: Alfred A. Knopf, 1965); D. W. Meinig, *The Great Columbia Plain: A Historical Geography, 1805–1910* (Seattle: University of Washington Press, 1968); David H. Stratton, "Hells Canyon: The Missing Link in Pacific Northwest Regionalism," *Idaho Yesterdays* 28 (Fall 1984): 3–9; Judith Austin, "Desert, Sagebrush, and the Pacific Northwest," in William G. Robbins et al., eds., *Regionalism and the Pacific Northwest* (Corvallis: Oregon State University Press, 1983), 129–47.

12. Richard White, *"It's Your Misfortune and None of My Own": A History of the American West* (Norman: University of Oklahoma Press, 1991), 487.

13. Henry Nash Smith, *Virgin Land: The American West as Symbol and Myth* (Cambridge, Mass.: Harvard University Press, 1950), 292. For more extensive comments on the concepts of frontier, region, and postregion, see Richard W. Etulain, *Re-Imagining the Modern American West: A Century of Fiction, History, and Art* (Tucson: University of Arizona Press, 1996). Consult, too, Richard W. Etulain, "Inventing the Pacific Northwest: Novelists and the Region's History," in *Terra Pacifica: People and Place in the Northwest States and Western Canada,* ed. Paul W. Hirt (Pullman: Washington State University Press, 1998), 25–52.

What Has Happened to the
Columbia? A Great River's Fate
in the Twentieth Century

BY WILLIAM L. LANG

$\mathcal{A}$t the end of the twentieth century and the dawn of a new millennium, the life of a great river has entered a dangerous phase. Reports from researchers and environmental watch groups warn that the magnificent and multi-millennial Columbia River may have been changed too much, accumulated too much pollution, or become so compromised that it has been indelibly transmogrified from a living river to an engineered, industrial sluice. Some declare the river critically unhealthy. They cite the decline in salmon returning to spawn in the Columbia and its tributaries and the federal government's use of the Endangered Species Act in 1992 to save the native Snake River sockeye salmon as symptoms of an ecological and political illness that may be fatal. Other warnings include documentation of industrial toxins and radioactive isotopes in the river and fundamental changes in water quality caused by logging and agricultural chemical run-offs. The future of the modern river, these reports suggest, is hanging in some kind of contingent but obscured balance, and it may be too late to avoid a regional catastrophe.[1]

The apocalyptic descriptions of the Columbia's future are matched by assurances from engineers and many scientists that what ails the river can be mitigated, remedied, and even reversed. Some deny that the Columbia is threatened in any serious way, arguing that while the river is a robust provider of human needs it is also perhaps the most scrutinized, monitored, and cared-for stream in North America. Nonetheless, federal and state governments have assiduously studied the Columbia—222 official reports were completed between 1956 and 1992—and have strenuously acted to mitigate the perceived problems. Between 1981 and 1996, for example, government agencies expended more than three billion dollars to protect wild salmon and improve fish runs. The Northwest Power Planning Council—mandated to monitor river management to equalize considerations afforded environmental, industrial, agricultural, and commercial concerns—has issued annual reports and drawn up several comprehensive plans for addressing the Columbia's problems. But no easy solutions have emerged. The industrial and agricultural users of the river, Indian tribes who fish and use the Columbia as guaranteed by treaty rights, recreational users, and environmental groups disagree about what should be done. Worse, the political process has put interest groups at odds over how and under what terms they can use the river. Underscoring their disagreements are strikingly different definitions of the river and depictions of its history, viewpoints that disclose fundamentally different understandings of what the Columbia means. The differences are buried deep in representations about history and place. This is where we should begin if we hope to sort out what has happened to the Columbia in our time.[2]

Writing about another place and another era in America's past, one of our nation's great poets put it exactly right when he characterized history as a relative of poetics, as a way of understanding the world that engages our curiosity, challenges our intelligence, and invokes our imagination.

> Historical sense and poetic sense should not, in the end, be contradictory, for if poetry is the little myth we make, history is the big myth we live, and in our living, constantly remake.[3]

Robert Penn Warren wrote these lines in reflection on the Civil War, but he could have been writing about our historical relationship with the Columbia River. It is a relationship that has been at the center of our lives in the Pacific Northwest for thousands of years, from the era when human groups first fished on the Columbia to the twentieth-century assault on the river to make it a generator of kilowatts, a source of irrigation water, a commercial conduit, and a playground. Throughout the history of our engagement with the river, there has been no clear line between what we have extracted from the river in material things and what the Columbia has meant to the spirit of the people. Because this division between the material and the spiritual has been so difficult to draw, our relationship with the river has been enigmatic, often as instrumental as spiritual, as inspirational as remunerative. In short, the Columbia is our largest living myth and the progenitor of a thousand other myths that we constantly have remade and have invited to remake us.

As a physical and environmental reality, the Columbia has been our life cord. The river's meaning to its human communities is embedded in the stories we have told about the river and especially in the images we have created to represent it. It has affected the human geography of our place more than any other force. We have settled by it, built towns along it, fished it, ridden it, siphoned it, bridged it, dammed it, and protected it. The Columbia is nothing if it is not a river that turbulently blends the historic and poetic senses. If what Robert Penn Warren wrote is correct, then how we have described, understood, and used the Columbia says as much about us as it does about the river. The corpus of stories we have created stands both as a catalog of our culture's mythic vision and as a measurement of the historically powerful effects of the Great River of the West.

The relationship between the Columbia and its people during this century has been more dynamic and disruptive than at any time in the past. Between the 1890s and the 1990s, human ingenuity physically altered the Columbia in ways that stagger. For millennia it had been a river so powerful that only vulcanism and catastrophic Pleistocene floods changed its course, but applied engineering has made it a mutant. Today's Columbia is characterized by massive impoundments, control gates and locks, and altered environments. The relationship between people and river during the twentieth century has been especially unequal, with the Columbia suffering and partially sacrificing itself to human desires. In the sketchiest history of the river, the Columbia's biography is recounted in measurements of sustenance or gain, its benefits calculated in fish caught, hydropower generated, and commerce tallied. In telling its more complex history, we know that the river has been given valuations other than its worth in the exchange of goods or as a provider of industrial energy. In these stories, the Columbia embodies the spiritual energy people desire from their environment, where human action participates in the broadest dramas of life. This story includes Native American tales of Coyote's distribution of salmon in the Columbia River Basin, descriptions by Euroamerican explorers of a pastoral and dangerous place, and an idealized river landscape protected by the 1986 Columbia River Gorge National Scenic Area Act. Making sense of the Columbia's fate during the twentieth century requires investigating these often contradictory perspectives.[4]

Two images dominate our views of the Columbia: the river as spiritual force and the river as cornucopian provider of economic value. At the center of both images is the Columbia's existence as nature. The raw and often terrible force of its current, the volume of its flow, and its extensive geologic and biotic environment make the Columbia a governing natural presence. Little that is natural or artificial within its 259,000-square-mile drainage area exists outside of the river's influence, from fish and wildlife to spinning turbines and barges transporting wheat. But what constitutes the natural and artificial on the Columbia, as historian Richard White recently argued, is a slippery conundrum; and once articulated, it raises additional questions about how we perceive the river as environment and human space. For twelve thousand years, the Columbia's environment has been the product of human and nonhuman forces, but during the last four decades the mixture has become much more dynamic and potentially confusing. Advocates to the new ecology, such as Daniel Botkin, argue that human-disturbed environments are little different in their components than their undisturbed counterparts. They are still places where natural processes and evolutionary dynamics operate and where flora and fauna exist in Darwinian niches and play out their lives. Our perceptions of the Columbia are no less contingent. From one angle, the river looks controlled and domesticated, prompting us to create images that are bold in engineering metaphors. From another angle, the river appears powerfully unpredictable, generative, and mesmerizing, which stimulates us to portray it in romantic, mystical, and even utopian terms.[5]

Images of the river as an economic and Edenic place run through the earliest Euroamerican descriptions of the Columbia. George Vancouver's men, in their fall 1792 survey of the river from the mouth to near modern-day Camas, Washington, wrote of the Columbia's pastoral beauty and commercial potential. Similarly, Meriwether Lewis and William Clark described the middle portion of the Columbia, from the mouth of the Snake River to present-day Astoria, Oregon, in terms that emphasized the fabulous wealth in anadromous fish and the clear opportunities for entrepreneurial investment. By the onset of "Oregon Fever" during the 1840s, the Columbia beckoned as wilderness environment and region for settlement, where Americans could extract wealth and establish homes. But it was the British Hudson's Bay Company that rushed to exploit the place, especially its fur-bearing animals. During the 1830s and 1840s, their descriptions and activities enhanced the Columbia's image as a cornucopia, where economic gain ruled human action, where, as geographer Cole Harris has argued, everything "turned around management, order, and property."[6] By mid-century, newly settled Americans in the Columbia River valley had extended the fur traders' reduction of the landscape to an ordered and commodified place, including the Oregon Steam Navigation Company's nearly monopolistic control of river passage from Portland to the Snake River. The image of the Columbia widened and lengthened through its identification with commerce to make it a political place, prompting Washington Territorial Governor Isaac Stevens to remark in 1860:

It is a matter of national defense, the development of our interior,
the availing ourselves of our geographical position. . . . It is not a
fiction, the great vision of Columbus. It is a fact that if we stand
firmly on our geographical position, and show a wise forecast in the
measures looking to the development of our country [Columbia
River Basin] we will have the means of diverting a large portion of
the trade of Asia, and causing it to flow through our own land.[7]

A strain of thought throughout the twentieth century reiterates
Stevens's representation of the Columbia as an economic destiny, a place
that contained the means for an enriching future. Beginning with the
first significant engineered alterations to the river during the 1880s and
1890s, the work of controlling the river increased in intensity and ac-
complishment throughout the twentieth century. As the work of building the first federal dams on the river got underway in 1933–1934, the
images of a controlled river defined the Columbia's benefits as both regionally and nationally strategic. Damming the Columbia and controlling the riverine environment, Portland river transportation company
owner Homer Shaver argued in 1934, "means the increasing of population here through the development of power and industries." The great
hydroelectric projects became the vehicle for modernity and for creation
of a new region in the basin. The prospect was both dynamic and benign.
The region would become dramatically energized while it would also create a new civilization that could avoid and correct the mistakes that already littered the nation's industrial history. "We will have small cities,"
Shaver prophesied, "with industries rather than large cities as in the
East." A decade later, during World War II, the images of a region electrified by falling water merged with visions of the Columbia as a cultural
savior and bulwark for the nation. Speaking in late 1943, Bonneville
Power Administration head Paul Raver pledged the river to a new future:

We are going to pay off our war debt. We are going to provide jobs
for returning men and soldiers coming home and people displaced

in their employment through this war. The harnessing of that resource—the river—is but a method, a device, if you please, for
paying off the mortgage—the war debt.[8]

This portrait of the Columbia takes instrumentality beyond commerce or defending regional wealth. In this vision, the river became a national property that could increase American prosperity and repay
Americans for sacrifices made during the war years. By the time the nation and region had adjusted to a peacetime economy, river managers
had revised their evaluations of the Corps of Engineers' earlier studies of
the Columbia's potential as a controlled waterway—the famous "308 Reports." A predicted power shortage, continued agitation by the transportation lobby for an "improved river," and the demand for more
irrigation impoundments led to authorization for McNary Dam near the
mouth of the Umatilla River. It was the beginning of a rationalized river,
where water in all tributaries would funnel into the mainstem to be used
by a growing number of claimants. It was also the beginning of the post-
New Deal construction of big dams on the Columbia that concluded in
1975, when the last of four dams on the lower Snake River went on line.
"It will be a rare drop of water," a government official remarked in 1949,
"which reaches the Columbia's broad mouth without having done some
useful work for the Northwest."[9]

Twin images of control and efficiency guided engineers on the Columbia. Falling water meant hydroelectric generation, while impounded
water meant transportation and storage for irrigation and flood control.
Dams could both drop water and impound it, and multipurpose dams
after World War II offered the promise that the Columbia would be a
willing servant of important economic constituencies and a friendlier
river that would stay within its banks. As the engineers stated clearly in
the revised "308 Report," the goal was a fully managed Columbia River
Basin that included numerous storage dams on tributaries and "run of
the river" dams on the Columbia and Snake. Engineers promised that
the new river would control or prevent the periodic and powerful flush-

ings that had been part of the great river system for thousands of years. During the nineteenth century alone, floods had drowned low areas in 1861, 1876, and 1894. The 1894 flood of record pushed 1,240,000 cubic feet per second past The Dalles. The river trickled by the same point in 1937 at only 36,000 cfs, the lowest documented flow on record. The image of a regulated river included eliminating these enormous swings and the seasonally erratic flow, which annually ran more than three times larger from May to August than from September to April. The engineers wanted to flatten out the river, to make it an equalized and regulated stream that could provide hydroelectricity on demand.[10]

Using the image of an engineered river knew few limits. Referring to anticipated difficulties in creating an integrated power network on the river in 1936, one engineer flatly promised: "There are no problems that cannot be solved, and their solution depends so completely on demands for power and their location, that preliminary planning is of rather academic value." It was an optimism that fueled itself on the seemingly limitless hydroelectric power that the Columbia offered. The future beckoned to the developers and to dreamers of an electrified river. Plans reified the dreams. Between 1931 and 1975, the Corps of Engineers conducted four major studies of the Columbia River Basin's navigable rivers and streams; other federal agencies completed another ten investigations that surveyed the region's riverine resources for development. Each plan concluded that mounds of data and sophisticated analyses proved the efficacy and rewards of operating the Columbia as a system, perhaps best as an improved natural system but nonetheless as a system. Increasingly, the evaluative measurement became economic. An extreme but not unrepresentative statement of this perspective appeared in the "Joint Policy Statement" issued by the negotiators of the U.S.-Canada Columbia River treaty in 1964:

> Cooperative development of the water resources of the Columbia
> River Basin, designed to provide optimum benefits to each country,
> requires that the storage facilities and downstream power produc-

tion facilities proposed by the respective countries will, to the extent it is practicable and feasible to do so, be added in order of the most favorable benefit-cost ratio.

After more than three decades of refining the system, the definition of the Columbia had edged toward a reality best expressed on graph paper, with lines of hydrological measurements intersecting those of kilowatt production and reservoir volumes.[11]

Despite the Columbia's apparent confiscation by the actuaries of modern engineering and hydroelectric development, other images had lived alongside these calculations and suggested a much different river. "Alone of all the rivers of the West," Samuel Bowles wrote in 1865, the Columbia

> has broken these stern barriers [mountains] and the theatre of the conquering conflict offers, as might naturally be supposed, many an unusual feature of nature, river and rock have striven together, wrestling in close and doubtful embrace—sometimes one gaining ascendancy, again the other but finally the subtler and seductive element worrying its rival out, and gaining the western sunshine, broken and scarred and foaming with hot sweat, but proudly victorious, and forcing the withdrawing arms of its opponent to hold up eternal moments of its triumph.

This image of power is no less impressive than the image of hydroelectric energy produced by spinning turbines a century later, but it is an organic strength that is depicted in a contested and natural drama. The image is both romantic and animistic, a portrait of the Columbia wrestling with its confining earthen structure to make its way to the sea. Seen from this viewpoint, there is blood, muscle, and heart in the river. For Bowles, the Columbia epitomized the raw and untamed nature that characterized the American West, a stereotypical image of exceptionalism that seems to emerge wholesale from the landscape.[12]

This Columbia—the romantic river—attracted investment of a different kind. By the end of the nineteenth century, when railroad and steamboat travel extended tourism to the Pacific West, the Columbia became part of a monumental landscape that exuded geographical and aesthetic power. The centerpiece was the 100-mile-long gorge that the Columbia had cut through the Cascade Mountains on its way to the Pacific. Towering cliffs, spectacular waterfalls, and a dense forest cover made it a place that prompted Scottish naturalist David Douglas in 1827 to call it "wild and romantic," a place that "is grand beyond description." By 1891, when regional historian Frances Fuller Victor wrote of the Columbia Gorge as a place where "wonder, curiosity, and admiration combine to arouse sentiments of awe and delight," Portland-based steamboats regularly cruised upriver to the Cascades with tourists who marveled as "each moment affords a fresh delight to the wondering senses."[13]

The river provided an inspiration that nearly matched its commercial potential. It seemed, as travel writer Henry Finck suggested in 1890, that nature had purposefully created the Gorge to embellish human life and improve health. Writing in *The Pacific Coast Tour*, Finck told readers he had "seen a great part of three continents,"

> but if I were asked what I considered the best investment of a five-dollar bill I had ever made for combined aesthetic enjoyment and hygienic exhilaration, I should name this return trip on the Columbia River. Tourists who have time for one trip only should go up the river, because in that direction the scenery is arranged most effectively, becoming ever grander and wilder till the climax is reached in the marvelous rapids above Dalles City.

This was landscape with purpose and dramatic effect. More than that, the river offered travelers an intimate connection with a domineering natural place, engendering awe and respect as well as aesthetic enjoyment. Steaming upriver into the Columbia's great, verdant gorge, large sternwheelers brought passengers and profits to steamboat companies. They also engaged an increasingly urbanized population in an intimate romance with a geography of scale so immense that it dwarfed human agency and a physical power so indomitable that it tested the steamboats' mechanical strength. Tourists always left the river impressed. The place overwhelmed in its open displays of emotional and psychological power. It compelled most commentators and publicists to plumb the mythic and mystic dimensions of human experience for descriptive analogs and comparisons, language to convey the inner strength of the place. Writers often located the source of the river's magical power deep in the land-scape itself. "Much has been written concerning the beauty of the Co-lumbia," a 1924 guidebook informed,

> but no word painting can adequately describe this masterpiece of nature's handiwork. There is a mystic beauty lurking in its vales and dells, which lifts the soul above the realms of time and space, and makes the beholder sense the presence of the divine.[14]

That sense of "the presence of the divine" on the Columbia coexisted with the depiction of the river as mundane but cornucopian. Through-out the twentieth century, these two distinctive images of the river en-gaged in a contingent relationship that defies easy characterization. It was not so much a tussle of contending visions as it was a dance of suit-ors who all desired a cultural claim on the river's future. It was in the pro-jections of imagined futures that the distinctions became sharpest, when the instrumentalist exploitation of the Columbia's power and riches di-verged strongly from the idealist preservation of the river's aesthetics and spirituality. But there were times when the two views overlapped and lines blurred, when development of the river merged human purpose with providence. Speaking at the dedication of The Dalles–Celilo Canal in 1915, Portland civic leader and investor Joseph Nathan Teal pressed both touchstones in his accolade to the creation of an artificial water-way around the great obstruction Lewis and Clark had called the "Long Narrows" and David Thompson had described as "this immense body of water under such compression, raging and hissing, as if alive." On May 5, 1915, Teal spoke enthusiastically under a hot sun to the largest crowd that had assembled in The Dalles since Oregon Trail days.

> This mighty work symbolizes the stern, unfaltering determination of the people that our waters shall be free—free to serve the uses and purposes of their creation by a Divine Providence. . . . It means the recognition by all that throughout this vast territory there is no division of interest. This a common country with a common purpose, a common destiny; and this stream, from its source to where it finally weds the ocean and is lost in the mighty Pacific, is one river—our river—in which we all have a common share.[15]

Mingled in the portrait Teal drew of the new canal, the powerful Columbia, and the future of the region were pictures of organic unity, the work of human ingenuity, divine purpose, and the merged fates of a river and its people. There is great cultural power in Teal's portrait, a communication that historian William Robbins has labeled a "celebratory breast beating" that became emblematic of the "instrumentalist designs of the dominant culture." It was that, but it was also more. For the power in Teal's imagery is in the wedding of the organic and the economic in the minds of his audience. No one could deny how the Columbia dominated in relationships between the river and its people, how the river's geography had provided opportunity for human activity and created obstacles to navigation. That was Teal's point when he proclaimed "that our waters shall be free—free to serve the uses and purposes of their creation by a Divine Providence." It was science and engineering, in other words, that allowed the Columbia to do what it could and what it should for humanity.[16]

The Columbia's instrumentalist future expanded well beyond Teal's imagination in 1915 and even the utility of the canal he helped dedicate. By the early 1920s, The Dalles–Celilo Canal had proven to be an economic failure. Nonetheless, for river developers like Teal and Nelson Blalock—who had told "Open Rivers Congress" in 1908 that creating an open river to Wenatchee could be "quickly and easily done" with a "few blasts"—the image of the Columbia as a thriving artery of commerce was a siren that continued to lure, culminating in the construction of dams on the lower Snake River more than fifty years later.[17]

As engineering changed the Columbia, however, the images of a natural environment continued to inform discussions and often provided countervalence to the drive to extract economic value from the river. During the first decade of big dam-building, for example, regional planners approached development on the Columbia as something of a trade-off between economic benefits and aesthetics. The location of Bonneville Dam provoked the issue, because it straddled the Columbia at the western end of the scenic Columbia Gorge and planners knew that low-cost electrical power could attract major industries to the site. The image of the great gorge forested with smokestacks rather than Douglas firs seemed appalling. B. H. Kizer, chairman of the Washington State Planning Commission in 1937, feared that once the dam began delivering low-cost power the Gorge would be "doomed and not all society's feeble contrivances can save it." The report of the planning commission echoed Kizer's warning:

> The introduction, into an area of great beauty, of that type of land use and construction which, of all the works of man, is least characterized by attractive appearance of architectural consideration, would be a visual incongruity which no subsequent effort could overcome. . . . The views from its summit [Beacon Rock] would overlook slag heaps and iron roofs, and all the miscellaneous jumble required by heavy chemical or metallurgical processing plants.[18]

In 1926, one of the seven commission members, highway builder Samuel C. Lancaster, had written a panegyric to the river which included: "The Columbia is peerless. Its grandeur speaks to men, and tells of Him who gathered the waters together into one place, and lifted up the mountains." The planners had a larger agenda. The likelihood of industrial developments in one of the most scenic portions of the river's mainstem forced them to ask difficult questions. Just what makes the Columbia special? What are the limits of development? What should be preserved or protected? The planning commission's Columbia Gorge Committee answered that their planning effort was not meant

> to restrict the play of the physical and economic forces released by the Bonneville project and the consequent inevitable developments in or near the Gorge, but to urge the parallel consideration of all of the social and economic forces and developments, and to protect real economic values involved in recreational facilities and scenery.[19]

The text of the committee's report reflected a measured evaluation of Bonneville Dam's potential to change the area and elevate the economic over the aesthetic. "If the unique scenic values of the Columbia Gorge are to survive," the planners concluded, "natural conditions and appearances must be largely retained." But they knew full well that preservation could go no further than protecting the landscape not affected by the dam itself. "The dam is calculated to serve future as well as present generations," their report surmised, "likewise, the Gorge if preserved, would be of continuing value." Their rationalizing planning process forced them to equate the "peerless" qualities of the river with economic valuations, suggesting that the Gorge "is a major asset to the surrounding territory" and "is of such importance that it may fairly be considered a national treasure for which the Federal government should manifest a protective concern." The benefits for people were manifest and manifold, but they had to be evaluated as economic assets, the "demonstrated power of attracting tourist travel . . . a large-scale income-bearing property," rather than as a contribution to public pleasure or a valued spiritual resource.[20]

Damming the Columbia compelled the river managers, especially the U.S. Army Corps of Engineers and the Bonneville Power Administration, to increasingly view the river as one vast plumbing system. The first run-of-the-river dams blocked the mainstem at the limits of flow within the United States at Bonneville and Grand Coulee. Additional dams, built by the federal government and public utility districts by the late 1960s, strung out between Bonneville and Grand Coulee, making the engineered Columbia the most productive hydroelectric river in the world and among the most controlled. The approval of the Columbia River Treaty between Canada and the United States in 1964 brought three additional mainstem dams on line by the mid-1970s. Completion of the lower Snake River dams and major storage dams on tributaries, such as Libby and Dworshak on the Kootenay and Clearwater rivers, filled out a system that required the daily regulation of water flows from more than two hundred fifty dams in the Columbia's drainage basin. In the plans of the river-manipulators, the purpose of the river could not be more obvious: "Every day this great river runs to the sea with any stretch of it unharnessed constitutes another day of wasted resources." [21] By the mid-1970s, engineers had "tamed" the Columbia by transmogrifying it from a predictably fluctuating river that flooded unpredictably and allowed water to flow "wasted" to the Pacific into a regulated stream understood best in acre-feet volumes in storage pools, feet of "head" behind dams, and millions of peak and "firm" kilowatts. It became what Richard White has called a "virtual river," a river represented in computer models created to predict salmon behavior in a Columbia that is littered with impediments and dangers for anadromous fish. In ways barely dreamed of by the planners during the 1930s, the refashioned Columbia had become the leading edge of the Pacific Northwest, the harbinger and vehicle for a braver new world. "The Columbia River of the future," an engineer prophesied in 1969, would become

> a model of resources development which will be the envy of the entire world. By then [1980s] sufficient new knowledge concerning migratory fish will exist to permit adjustment of the now rigid water quality standards. . . . for a revitalized salmon industry, and for a high quality municipal supply.[22]

As magnificent as that imagined future might have seemed in 1969, there was a down side that the engineer acknowledged in his vision of the new river—the critical decline in anadromous fish runs in the mainstem and tributaries. No image of the manipulated river is bleaker or more disheartening than a Columbia without salmon fighting their way upstream to spawning beds, some swimming more than nine hundred miles and climbing more than sixty-five hundred feet from the ocean. That picture is the verso of the brilliant image of spinning turbines and the high-voltage transmission of low-cost electricity throughout the Pacific Northwest and as far south as southern California. This Janus-faced portrait of the modern Columbia represents both a vexing conundrum for Pacific Northwesterners and a battleground over what the river means to the human community.

From the earliest descriptions of the great river, the symbol of riverine fecundity had been the teeming millions of salmon that swam upriver in seasonal runs. Lewis and Clark had described a river "Crouded with Salmon in maney places" and reported sightings of "emence quantities of fish" near the mouth of the Snake River in their 1805 descent of the Columbia. The estimates of migrating salmon invited exaggeration and fantastic stories, but the exceptional harvests by commercial fishers using seines, traps, and fishwheels seemed to justify the tales. A fishwheel at Cascade Locks scooped up 54,000 pounds of salmon in one day in 1894, and fifty years later a seine operated at The Dalles caught 70,000 pounds in a single day. The image of fecundity beyond belief had its penultimate expression in one of the great stories often repeated on the river and recorded by Patrick Donan in 1898:

> Citizen George Francis Train, many years ago, left this statement—that would be remarkable anywhere else: "This is to certify, that I have today, with my slippers on, walked across the Columbia River, at The Dalles of Oregon, on the backs of the salmon, without getting my feet wet;—Colonel N. B. Sinott was a witness of the feat."[23]

Salmon migrating up the Columbia became vulnerable to nets and spears at Celilo Falls, where native fishers had garnered one-third of their annual caloric needs from the Columbia for thousands of years. They caught perhaps as much as 18 million pounds each year from six seasonal runs. Among pre-contact fisheries in North America none was more productive than at the series of rapids, basalt cliffs, and falls that curved across the river at Celilo. And at no place did salmon so dominate the lives of native peoples. Because of the singular importance of salmon, Indian fishers honored the captured fish through elaborate ceremonies. Each year at the first catch, Yakama fishers deposited the bones of the first salmon on the river bottom as a beckoning to the millions of salmon to follow. The ceremony recognized the ecological character of salmon behavior and signified the people's gratitude for the salmon's sacrifice. "They came to provide us an example of sacrifice," Yakama leader Ted Strong has reminded, "and we thank the creator that gave the salmon the feeling of servitude." [24]

In the late twentieth century, the fate of the salmon has become a litmus test of the river's ecological health, and salmon have become an icon for all that is natural and spiritual in the Columbia. The picture of salmon swimming against strong current or leaping waterfalls confirms the specialness of this animal, while it also characterizes the river's power in a way quite different from the image of a revolving turbine. Although Indian people have always revered salmon, it was not until the numbers of migrating fish went into a steep decline after the mainstem dams were built that non-Indians made salmon iconographic. The closing off of fish habitat by the dams—especially in the streams made inaccessible to fish by Grand Coulee Dam—combined with increasing commercial fisheries in the rivers and the ocean and the spoilating consequences of agriculture, timber, and industry to push salmon stocks to the edge of extinction. Fisheries biologists such as Joseph Craig had warned about these consequences as early as 1935, but the river managers made their choices regardless of the caveats. By 1947, with Bonneville and Grand Coulee in place and plans for three additional dams on the drawing boards, one official wrote: "It is, therefore, the conclusion of all concerned that the overall benefits to the Pacific Northwest from a thorough-going development of the Snake and Columbia are such that the present salmon run must be sacrificed." The trade-off could not be more simply stated. Dams and development, the economic river, triumphing over salmon, the natural and spiritual river. Dams became the contrary icon to salmon, the personification of a damaged environment and altered relationships with the river. There was enthusiasm for dams as symbols of progress and improved living conditions, but there was also anger at what the dams killed in the river and how they inundated the past. Yakama leader Bill Yallup remembered tribal members standing on a hill above Celilo watching the river cover the falls: "Some of them sang songs like a funeral. They were very sacred songs. Three days and nights with no sleep. It was a sad day for them." Others acted out their concern. When the Corps of Engineers began preparing for The Dalles Dam, a young Ed Edmo remembered joining with other Indian boys to register an objection: "When the workmen finished surveying at the end of the day, some of us would pull out the stakes from the ground, fill the holes, and make a small fire out of the stakes. . . . In our own small way, we tried to stop the dam." Edmo and his friends knew they could not win. Nothing could stop the dams.[25]

By the 1980s, when the clarion call sounded to stem the decline of salmon runs, the dams became the focus of harsh criticism from nearly everyone who wanted the Columbia full of salmon again. Each group that contends for control of the river's future reaches back for historical justification of its wishes. Fishers bemoan the changes that have diminished salmon, and they long for a return to a river more congenial to their pursuits. Tribal governments, using the power inherent in their treaties and confirmed in recent court decisions, remind government agencies and private concerns that all changes that deprive them of access to salmon in the river and diminish salmon violate their heritage and religion. The dams, by casting themselves as "the future river," sharply abandon history and seem to stand outside of the river's historical narrative. Their existence literally swamps the past and verges on desecrating what remains. To embrace the river's past, in some sense, is to challenge the dams and to question the Columbia's future. And it is anything but a romantic past, as lower Columbia fisherman Kent Martin's comments make clear: "Everything people said in the 1940s is coming true like a curse." Portrayed in these ways, the Columbia's story invites historicizing and polemics. Nonetheless, the most powerful narrative is found in representations of how the river has shaped the human condition and how human actions have shaped the modern river. The public seems to identify with both the economic and the spiritual Columbia. Opinion polls consistently reflect popular support for "saving the salmon," but they also indicate that people hesitate to change the management of the river without guaranteed results. At the end of the twentieth century, the story of the Columbia has become an inescapable conundrum.[26]

The compelling mythic story, even in the face of the most difficult choices, is a miraculous blend of both views of the river. In 1959, for example, the Oregon League of Women Voters addressed the threats to the Columbia in a widely distributed pamphlet:

> Even with the abundance of water in the Columbia there already have arisen certain conflicts in use, as for instance between fish and power. It is not likely, however, that it will happen here as that which has occurred in some other sections of the country—we shall have to decide: fish or power! We can still have water for humans and fish, water for crops and forests, unspoiled streams for esthetic appreciation and water for fun IF, through comprehensive planning, the right choices and compromises are made in time.[27]

The compromises boil down to the conflict underscored by the League of Women Voters in 1959: Will it be fish or power? In each strategy devised by river managers and fisheries experts since 1959, promises of sufficient water for both fish and power have been constants. Neither view has been abandoned. As recently as 1993, Representative Ron Wyden commented on how the Columbia should be protected from degradation:

> For people on both sides of the river, the Columbia is much more
> than a transportation route. For generations, the Columbia has
> been a source of exploration, inspiration and recreation. . . . We can
> either make some targeted investments right now or pay more in
> the long run.

The investments have been incredible, yet the solution to preserving the
spiritual and historic river continues to elude us. The previously un-
imaginable strategy of removing dams has emerged from planning meetings into the full light of day. Tribal representatives want fish in the
Columbia, while power and water users hope they can retain their claim
on the river. The discussion, the story, and the expensive remediations
roll on like the river itself, with no one quite sure how to stop the flow
and decide which river to enshrine. "Either we ought to make enough
changes to give the salmon a chance of coming back," former Northwest
Power Planning Council Chairman Angus Duncan concluded, "or we
shouldn't be spending any of this money at all." Yet, the will to have both
power and salmon drive the storyline hard. In the political arena, the two
goals remain joined, the two rivers still flow together. Oregon Governor
John Kitzhaber put it bluntly: "You can't solve power issues without solving the fish issues, and you can't solve the fish issues without solving the
power issues." [28]

This is part of the myth that pervades the Pacific Northwest, a part
that runs rich in Robert Penn Warren's historic and poetic senses. For the
Columbia, the myth is a mixed blessing at best, while for the people of
the Columbia it is simply how the river is understood. There are few children of the region who do not have both rivers flowing through them;
there are few who are entirely immersed in the economic or the spiritual
river. It is what makes the questions about the Columbia's future so
intractable. No one is quite free of the power of the competing visions of
the river. Nonetheless, in the Pacific Northwest, the Columbia River has
given life to all. Oregon novelist and poet H. L. Davis put it just right in
his "Rivers to Children":

We rivers, we torrents,
We heavy-backed waters
Browned out of the green ocean,
Came, clouds, from the plunging
Sea restless as flame.
One-willed and unchanging,
We rained and flowed westward.
We crossed these same meadows.
We touched and knew children
Like you; not the same.[29]

What has happened to the Columbia River during the twentieth century has happened to the entire region. Like the river that has been changed so much, none of us is quite the same.

NOTES

1. For discussions of the crisis on the Columbia, see Joseph Cone, *A Common Fate: Endangered Salmon and the People of the Pacific Northwest* (New York: Henry Holt, 1995); Kai N. Lee, *Compass and Gyroscope: Integrating Science and Politics for the Environment* (Washington, D.C.: Island Press, 1993), esp. chap. 2; William L. Lang, "River of Change: Salmon, Time, and Crisis on the Columbia River," in *The Northwest Salmon Crisis: A Documentary History*, ed. Joseph Cone and Sandy Ridlington (Corvallis: Oregon State University Press, 1996): 348–63. On radioactive nuclides, see Hanford Health Information Network, "Potential Health Problems from Exposure to Selected Radionuclides" (Olympia: Washington State Department of Health, 1994), and http://www.doh.wa.gov/hanford/.

2. For a recent discussion of the effort to save salmon on the Columbia, see the pro–Corps of Engineers study, Lisa Mighetto and Wes Ebel, *Saving the Salmon* (Seattle: HRA, 1994), and Jonathan Brinckman, "$3 Billion Later, Columbia Basin Salmon Dwindle," *Oregonian*, July 27, July 28, 1997.

3. Robert Penn Warren, *Brother to Dragons: A Tale in Verse and Voices*, ix, quoted in Michael Kammen, *Mystic Chords of Memory: The Transformation of Tradition in American Culture* (New York: Vintage Books, 1991), 29.

4. For discussions of the Native American landscape, see Eugene Hunn, *Nich'i-Wána "The Big River": Mid-Columbia Indians and Their Land* (Seattle:

University of Washington Press, 1990), and Jarold Ramsay, *Coyote Was Going There: Indian Literature of the Oregon Country* (Seattle: University of Washington Press, 1979). For the Columbia River Gorge, see Carl Abbott, Sy Adler, and Margery Post Abbott, *Planning a New West: The Columbia River Gorge National Scenic Area* (Corvallis: Oregon State University Press, 1997).

5. Richard White, *The Organic Machine* (New York: John Wiley, 1995), esp. chap. 1. On the new ecology, see Daniel Botkin, *Discordant Harmonies: A New Ecology for the Twenty-First Century* (New York: Oxford, 1990).

6. Cole Harris, *The Resettlement of British Columbia: Essays on Colonialism and Geographical Change* (Vancouver: University of British Columbia Press, 1997), 34. For discussion of HBC and views about nature, see Elizabeth Vibert, *Traders' Tales: Narratives of Cultural Encounters in the Columbia Plateau, 1807–1846* (Norman: University of Oklahoma Press, 1997), 19–21.

7. Isaac Stevens, speaking in Vancouver, Washington Territory, May 20, 1860, in the *Pioneer and Democrat* (Olympia, Washington), May 23, 1860. On the Columbia and early historical descriptions, see William L. Lang, "Creating the Columbia: Historians and the Great River of the West, 1890–1935," *Oregon Historical Society Quarterly* 93 (Fall 1992): 235–62. For a thorough discussion of American settlement and its effects on the environment in the lower Columbia River region, see Robert Bunting, *The Pacific Raincoast: Environment and Culture in an American Eden, 1778–1900* (Lawrence: University Press of Kansas, 1997), esp. chap. 7.

8. Homer T. Shaver, comments at IEWA Board Meeting, Wenatchee, Washington, October 20, 1934, and Paul Raver, address to IEWA Convention, Lewiston, Idaho, October 9, 1943, Inland Empire Waterways Association Collection, Pacific Northwest and Whitman College Archives, Whitman College, Walla Walla, Washington. For discussion of similar arguments, see White, *Organic Machine*, 64–70.

9. Quoted in Murray Morgan, *The Columbia* (Seattle: Superior, 1949), 283.

10. Gus Norwood, *Columbia River Power for the People: A History of Policies of the Bonneville Power Administration* (Portland, Ore.: Bonneville Power Administration, 1981), 180–1; J. A. Krug, *The Columbia: A Comprehensive Report on the Development of Water Resources of the Columbia River Basin* (Washington, D.C.: Bureau of Reclamation, 1947), 274–5; White, *Organic Machine*, 76–7.

11. H. V. Carpenter to Marshall N. Dana, January 6, 1936, Pacific Northwest River Basins Commission Papers, Box 41, RG 315, NARS, Pacific Northwest Branch, Seattle, Washington; John V. Krutilla, *The Columbia River Treaty: The Economics of an International River Basin Development* (Baltimore: Johns Hopkins University Press, 1967), 60. For a list of Columbia River Basin plans, see

"Briefing on Columbia River Tributaries," September 17, 1975, Pacific Northwest River Basins Commission Papers, Box 29.

12. Samuel Bowles, *Across the Continent: A Summer's Journey to the Rocky Mountains, the Mormons, and the Pacific States* (New York: Hurd & Houghton, 1865), 185–6.

13. David Douglas, *Memoir of the Late Mr. David Douglas* (London, 1901), 104; Frances Fuller Victor, *Atlantis Arisen, or Talks of a Tourist about Oregon and Washington* (Philadelphia: J. B. Lippincott, 1891), 54, 55, quoted in Abbott et al., *Planning a New West*, 1, 5.

14. Henry T. Finck, *The Pacific Coast Tour* (New York: Charles Scribner's Sons, 1890), 189; J. H. & J. F. Oppenlander, *The Columbia River Guide and Panorama, From Portland to The Dalles* (Portland: J. H. Oppenlander, 1924), 1.

15. J. B. Tyrell, ed., *David Thompson: Narrative of His Explorations in Western America, 1784–1812* (Toronto: Champlain Society, 1916), 496–7; "Address of Joseph Nathan Teal, The Dalles–Celilo Celebration, Big Eddy, Oregon, May 5, 1915," *Oregon Historical Quarterly* 16 (Fall 1916): 107–8.

16. William G. Robbins, "The World of Columbia River Salmon: Nature, Culture, and the Great River of the West," in *Northwest Salmon Crisis*, ed. Cone and Ridlington, 14.

17. Nelson Gates Blalock, "Address to Open Rivers Congress," Wenatchee Commercial Club, Wenatchee, 1908, Nelson Gates Blalock Papers, Cage 1644, Washington State University Library Special Collections, Pullman. On continuing desire for navigation improvements, see Lang, "River of Change," 354–7.

18. B. H. Kizer to Washington State Planning Board, January 1937; Gorge Committee of the Pacific Northwest Regional Planning Commission, *Report on the Problem of Conservation and Development of Scenic and Recreational Resources of the Columbia Gorge in Washington and Oregon* (Portland: PNWRPC, 1937), 17–18. For additional context and discussion, see Abbott et al., *Planning a New West*, 34–7.

19. Samuel C. Lancaster, *The Columbia: America's Great Highway* (Portland: J. K. Gill, 1926), 1; *Report on the Problem of Conservation*, ix.

20. *Report on the Problem of Conservation*, 20–1, 28, 32.

21. Committee on Interior and Insular Affairs, *Upper Columbia River Development*, 84th Cong., 2d sess. Rept. No. 2831 (Washington: GPO, 1956), 1–2. The statements quoted are the comments of Senator James Murray of Montana.

22. White, *Organic Machine*, 106; Robert T. Jaske, "Columbia River of the Future," MS of a speech delivered in Richland, Washington, April 15, 1969, 5–6, VF 2233, Washington State University Special Collections, Pullman.

23. Gary Moulton, ed., *The Journals of the Lewis and Clark Expedition*, vol. 5 (Lincoln: University of Nebraska Press, 1988), 286, 298; William Ashley to President Andrew Jackson, in *Message from the President . . . relative to the Columbia*, 21st Cong., 2d sess., Ex. Doc. 1, 1831 (Serial Set 203), 18; Patrick Donan, *The Columbia River Empire* (Portland: Oregon Railroad and Navigation Company, 1898), 59. For Columbia River fisheries statistics, see Courtland Smith, *Salmon Fishers of the Columbia* (Corvallis: Oregon State University Press, 1979).

24. Ted Strong, quoted in *Los Angeles Times*, February 23, 1997, 5. On the importance of salmon and the first-salmon ceremony, see Hunn, *Nich'i-Wána*, 148–54; Robert T. Boyd, *People of The Dalles: The Indians of Wascopam Mission* (Lincoln: University of Nebraska Press, 1996), 127–9.

25. Memo, Julius Krug, Acting Chairman of Interior Department's Pacific Northwest Coordination Committee, March 6, 1947, RG 48, Records Concerning Regional Field Committees, Box 19, Entry 887, National Archives, Washington, D.C.; Bill Yallup, quoted in *Los Angeles Times*, February 3, 1997, 5; Ed Edmo, "After Celilo," in *Talking Leaves: Contemporary Native American Short Stories*, ed. Craig Lesley (New York: Laurel, 1991), 71–2. For a critique of salmon as a regional icon, see John M. Findlay, "A Fishy Proposition: Regional Identity in the Pacific Northwest," in *Many Wests: Place, Culture, and Regional Identity*, David M. Wrobel and Michael C. Steiner (Lawrence: University of Kansas Press, 1997), 37–70.

26. Kent Martin, quoted in *Mother Earth News*, August 1, 1994.

27. Oregon League of Women Voters, "Our Columbia River" (Portland: Oregon Historical Society, 1959).

28. Ron Wyden, quoted in *The Oregonian*, March 23, 1993; Angus Duncan and John Kitzhaber, quoted in *The Oregonian*, July 27, 1997.

29. H. L. Davis, "Rivers to Children," in *Selected Poems* (Boise: Ahsahta Press, 1978), 26.

Contributors

Robert C. Carriker is professor of history at Gonzaga University and author of *Father Peter John De Smet: Jesuit in the West* (University of Oklahoma Press, 1995).

Richard W. Etulain is professor of history at the University of New Mexico, Director of the Center for the American West, and author of *Re-Imagining the Modern American West: A Century of Fiction, History, and Art* (University of Arizona Press, 1996).

Eugene S. Hunn is professor of anthropology at the University of Washington and author of *Nich'i-Wána, "The Big River": Mid-Columbia Indians and Their Land* (University of Washington Press, 1990).

William L. Lang is professor of history at Portland State University, Director of the Center for Columbia River History, and author of *Confederacy of Ambition: William Winlock Miller and the Making of Washington Territory* (University of Washington Press, 1996).

William D. Layman is a family counselor and local historian in Wenatchee, Washington, and author of articles on upper Columbia River exploration and rock art in *Columbia, the Magazine of Northwest History*.

Patricia Nelson Limerick is professor of history at the University of Colorado, author of *The Legacy of Conquest* (W. W. Norton, 1987) and co-author of *The Frontier in American Culture* (University of California Press, 1996).

James P. Ronda is Barnard Professor of history at the University of Tulsa and author of *Lewis and Clark among the Indians* (University of Nebraska Press, 1984) and *Astoria and Empire* (University of Nebraska Press, 1990).

Lillian Schlissel is Director of American Studies at Brooklyn College and author of *Women's Diaries of the Westward Journey* (Schocken Books, 1982) and co-author of *Far from Home: Families of the Westward Movement* (Schocken Books, 1989).

Henry Zenk is an anthropologist and linguistic specialist in Portland, Oregon, and author of articles about Willamette Valley Indians in the Smithsonian's *Handbook of North American Indians: Northwest Coast*.

Index

Abbott, Carl, 15

Abbott, Margery, 15

Adler, Sy, 15

Agee, James, 87

Alaska, 81

Albright, Mary Ann: in Illinois, 114, 116, 117–8; descendants of, 118

Albuquerque, NM, 120

Alexie, Sherman,138

Amtrak: in Columbia River Gorge, 85

Archaeology: at Columbia Plateau sites, 20, 24, 62, 64, 66. *See also* Rock art

Army Corps of Engineers, U.S.: as agent of change on Columbia River, 92, 157–8; reports on Columbia River, 150, 151

Arrowsmith, Aaron, 83

Astor, John Jacob, 84, 92

Astoria, OR: as site of first Columbia River centennial, 35, 42–3; estab-lished, 37; mentioned, 9, 14, 45, 92, 148. *See also* Fort Astoria

Astorians, 38, 93, 100, 127

Athabasca River, 81

Atomic Energy Commission, 104

Austin, Judith, 139

Baker's Bay, WA, 43, 101, 103

Balch, Frederic Homer, 127–9

Bancroft, Hubert Howe, 130–1

Barlow, Samuel, 10

Barrow, Susan, 64, 66

Beacon Rock, 156

Beckham, Stephen Dow, 122

Beinecke Rare Book and Manuscript Library, 118

Belyea, Barbara, 14

Benton, Thomas Hart (artist), 135

Benton, Thomas Hart (senator), 132

Berry, Wendell, 76, 88, 122

Biles, John, 115, 117, 118

Binns, Archie, 135

Blackfoot Indians, 23

Blalock, Nelson, 156

Boldt, George, 8, 29, 31, 32

Bonneville Dam: influence on Columbia River Gorge, 156, 160; mentioned, 84, 86, 140

Bonneville Power Administration: named, 92; mentioned, 53, 149, 157

Botkin, Daniel, 147–8

Bowles, Samuel, 152

Boyd, Robert, 14

Brand, Max, 132

Brautigan, Richard, 138

Bretz Flood, 20

Bridal Veil Falls, 130

Bridge of the Gods, 127, 128

Broughton, William Robert: crosses Columbia River Bar, 98–9; contacts Native Americans, 106–7; on beauty of Columbia, 148; mentioned, 10, 95

Buck, Rex, 75

Buffalo, 59, 77

Buffalo, NY, 120

Bunyan, John, 92

Bureau of Reclamation, U.S.: as agent of change on Columbia River, 92

Burlington Northern–Santa Fe Railroad, 85

Cabinet Rapids on Columbia River, 54, 70

Cain, Thomas, 62, 70

California gold rush, 95

Callenbach, Ernest, 138

Camas, 22

Campbell, John, 62

Canals: at Erie, NY, 89; at Cape Disappointment, WA, 103–4; at The Dalles, OR, 154–5

Carson River, 89

Carver, Jonathan, 80, 81, 83

Cascades of Columbia River. *See* Long Narrows of Columbia River

Cayuse Indians, 26, 27

Celilo Falls of Columbia River. *See* The Dalles–Celilo Falls complex

Celilo Indians, 19

Census reports, 119, 120

Centennial of Columbia River: first celebration of, 35, 42–3

Center for Columbia River History, 5

Chatham (sloop-of-war), 98–99

Chehalis (barkentine), 42

Chehalis Indians, 36

Chief Joseph Dam, 24

China: trade with, 80, 85, 127, 132

Chinookan: as language, 19. *See also* Chinook Indians; Chinook Jargon

Chinook Indians: language of, 36–37; in first Columbia River centennial, 43; and Pacific-Plateau trade network, 77, 78

Chinook Jargon: as trade language, 9, 39–40; formation of, 36; history of, 37–8; used by family households, 39; alphabet and cadence of, 44–5; examples of, 45–50, 93–4, 105, 50n2, 51n13, 52n16–20

Clark County, OR, 119

Clark Fork River, 4

Clark's Landing. *See* The Dalles, OR

Clark, William, 77

Clatsop Indians, 37

Clovis Point, 8, 20

Coast Guard, U.S.: station at Cape Disappointment, 104–5
Cody, Robin, 14
Cohen, Fay, 4
Colorado River, 89, 90
Coluee City, WA, 129
Columbia River: defined, 3–4; literature on, 3–5, 10–15, 127–39; major tributaries of, 4; environmental conditions on, 4; and "Ouragon" River, 9, 80–1, 82, 83; as borderland, 10; first centennial of, 35, 42–3; fur trade on, 37, 84, 85, 87; as soul of a region, 76–7; and imperial dreams, 80–4; wheat transported on, 84, 85; importance of, 89; compared to Colorado River, 90; named, 91; political significance of, 107–8; as both unifying and dividing force, 126–7, 131–2, 141; as area ripe for civilization, 127–8; river towns of, 129–30, 133–4; as developing region, 136–7; recent views on, 137–9, 144; official reports on, 145, 150, 151; as spiritual force, 147; as economic destiny, 147–50; as epitome of untamed nature, 152. *See also* Columbia River Bar; Gray, Robert; "Ouragon River"
Columbia Basin Project, 136
Columbia Basin Rock Hounds Club, 70
Columbia Indians: homelands of, 56
Columbia Plateau: floods create, 8, 146; style of rock art, 56, 66
Columbia Rediviva (ship), 42, 47, 91
Columbia River Archaeological Society, 71, 73
Columbia River Bar: crossing of, 10, 92, 94, 96–105

Columbia River Bar Pilots Association, 104, 109
Columbia River Basin: development of, 4; earliest human presence in, 8; mentioned, 126, 147
Columbia River Gorge: Oregon Trail in, 3, 10; Pleistocene floods in, 8, 146; reports on dams in, 156–7; mentioned, 77, 153
Columbia River Gorge National Scenic Area, 15, 147
Columbus, Christopher, 5, 23, 81
Combe, William, 82
Concomly (Chinook), 39
Cone, Joseph, 13
Confederated Tribes of the Colville Reservation, 56
Confederated Tribes of the Grand Ronde Community of Oregon: reservation of, 40; speakers of Chinook Jargon, 44, 50n8, 51n15
Confederated Tribes of the Umatilla Indian Reservation, 41
Confederated Tribes of Warm Springs Reservation, 19, 30, 41
Cook, James, 81
Cook's Inlet, AK, 81
Cook's River, 81, 82
Cowlitz River, 4
Coyote (Spilyay): mythical stories about, 19, 20–1, 147
Craig, Joseph, 160–1
Cressman, Luther, 20
Crosby, Arthur, 23–4
Cundy, Harold: documents rock art, 58, 64, 66, 70, 73, 74
Curlew, Billie, 60
Curry, John Steuart, 136

D'Antonio, Michael, 12

Dalles. *See* The Dalles

Dams: on Columbia River, 9, 18, 20, 21, 54, 60, 62, 64, 70, 86, 90, 140, 150, 156, 158–61; on Snake River, 13, 150, 156, 158; archaeological sites at, 24, 60, 62, 64, 71, 74; on Colorado River, 90; on Clearwater and Kootenay rivers, 158. *See also* Engineering; Grand Coulee Dam

Davis, Harold Lenoir, 133–4, 163–4

Deane, Al, 64

Denver, 94, 120

Department of Energy, 104

Deschutes River, 4

Diaries. *See* Journals

Dietrich, William, 11–2

Disappointment, Cape, 92, 96, 103–4

Discovery (sloop-of-war), 81

Disease: influence on Indians, 25. *See also* Smallpox

Dodds, Gordon, 139

Doig, Ivan, 137–8

Donan, Patrick, 159

Douglas Creek on Columbia River, 70

Douglas, David, 153

Duncan, Angus, 163

Dworshak Dam, 158

East Wenatchee, WA: Clovis point found at, 8; rock art at, 9

Ebel, Wes, 13

Edmo, Ed, 161

Ehrlich, Gretel, 76

Eliot, T. S., 77

Ellensburg, WA, 126

Endangered Species Act: and salmon, 144

Engineering: of Columbia River, 11, 12,

13, 14, 85, 140, 146, 149, 156, 157–8. *See also* Bonneville Power Administration; Northwest Power Planning Council; *individual dams*

Etulain, Richard, 10–1

Exploration. *See* Pacific Ocean; *names of individual explorers*

Faragher, John Mack, 120

Finck, Henry, 153

First Peoples of the Columbia. *See* Native Americans

Fish runs: in Columbia River, 3, 4, 53, 130; judicial decisions on, 8, 29, 31–2; influenced by dams, 91. *See also* Salmon

Fisher, Vardis, 135, 137

Fivemile Rapids of Columbia River: archaeological excavations at, 20

Flathead Indians, 23

Floods: on Columbia River, 151

Forde, G. B., 14

Fort Astoria, 37, 39, 84. *See also* Astoria, OR

Fort Cascades, WA, 116

Fort Clatsop, OR, 84

Fort George. *See* Fort Astoria

Fort Stevenson, OR, 42

Fort Vancouver, WA: languages used at, 39–40; located near Malick homestead, 115, 116, 117; mentioned, 40, 41, 84

Fox, Mr. (officer on *Tonquin*), 100–1, 102, 103

Fraser River, 82

Fredin, Adeline, 56

Frémont, John C., 107–8, 109

Fuller, George W., 136

Fur trade: on Columbia River, 3, 9,

37, 38, 84, 85, 148; use of Chinook
Jargon, 36, 39

Gates, Charles M., 136–7
Gerber, Michelle Stenjehem, 12
Giamatti, Bart, 122–3
Gibson, James, 14
Ginko Petrified Forest State Park, WA,
64
Grand Coulee Dam: building of, 91, 135;
influence on Columbia River, 158,
160; mentioned, 84, 86, 136, 140
Grand Coulee of Columbia River, 20,
60
Grant County, WA, Public Utility Dis-
trict, 62, 64
Gray, Robert: enters Columbia River, 5,
9, 14, 35, 42, 48, 50, 82, 88, 97, 98, 127;
names Columbia River, 91; men-
tioned, 95, 106
Grays Bay, WA, 48
Grays Harbor Indians, 43
Great River of the West conference:
sponsors, 5; content of, 8–11; Co-
lumbia River literature published
since, 11–5
"Great River of the West." See Colum-
bia River
Greengo, Robert, 62, 70
Grey, Zane, 132
Gros Ventre. See The Dalles, OR
Grosvenor, Thomas, 64
Guterson, David, 138
Guthrie, A. B., Jr., 137–8
Guthrie, Woody, 85–7

Hale, Horatio, 39–40
Hale, Janet Campbell, 138
Hanford Nuclear Engineering Works:

literature about, 12–3, 140; waste
management for, 108–9; mentioned,
53
Hanford Reach of Columbia River, 92
Harden, Blaine, 13
Harris, Cole, 148
Harrison, Joseph, 139
Hawksbills Point, WA, 74
Haycox, Ernest,137, 139
Henry, Andrew, 93
Hevly, Bruce, 12
Holbrook, Stewart, 138
Holmes, Brian, 70
Holmes, Susan, 70
Hood, Mount, 10
Hood River, OR, 14, 127
Horse Heaven Hills, WA, 22
Horse: myths about, 21–2; as rock art
image, 59
Horsethief Lake State Park, WA, 54
Howard, Joseph Kinsey, 139
Howison, Neil M.: crosses Columbia
River Bar, 97, 109–10; mentioned, 95
Hudson River, 83
Hudson's Bay Company: trade on Co-
lumbia River, 14, 26, 148; at Fort
Vancouver, 39; mentioned, 3, 40,
102
Humboldt River, 89
Hunn, Eugene, 8, 77
Hydroelectricity. See Engineering

Illinois, 114, 116, 120
Indans. See Native Americans
Indian reservations: significance of, 29–
30, 33; mentioned, 19, 40, 41. See also
Yakima Indians
Insanity, 117, 120–1
Ives, Joseph Christmas, 90

Jackson, Andrew, 103

James River, 83

Japan, 14, 132

Jefferson, Thomas, 82, 83, 86, 122

Jim, Howard, 19, 20, 31

Johansen, Dorothy O., 136–7

Johnson, Dorothy, 137

Jones, Nard, 11, 135

Journals: of overland trails, 112

Kamiakan, 27, 28

Kelly, Elizabeth, 118

Kesey, Ken, 138

Kip, Lawrence, 27–8

Kipling, Rudyard, 130

Kittitas Indians, 56

Kitzhaber, John, 163

Kizer, B. H., 156

Klamath Indians, 41

Klickitat Indians, 19

Kootenay River, 4

Lake Missoula flood, 20

Lancaster, Samuel C., 156

Lavender, David, 138

Layman, William, 8–9

Lee, Kai, 15

Lesley, Craig, 11, 138

Letters. *See* Journals

Lewis and Clark Expedition: encounter
    Native Americans, 18–25 passim; de-
    scribe Pacific-Plateau trade network,
    77; encounter Pacific Ocean, 95–6;
    describe environment of middle Co-
    lumbia River, 148, 154; on salmon,
    159; mentioned, 3, 83, 84, 85, 95, 127

Lewis River, 4

Lewiston, ID, 93

Libby Dam, 158

Limerick, Patricia, 10, 140

Literature: of Columbia River, 3–5,
    10–5, 127–39; oral, 8; on Hanford
    Nuclear Engineering Works, 12–3;
    on salmon, 13; of Columbia river
    towns, 129–30, 133–5, 152–3

Long Narrows of Columbia River: style
    of rock art, 56; and Pacific-Plateau
    trade network, 77, 78; described, 78,
    154–5

Looking Glass (Nez Perce), 27

Lopez, Barry, 82

Lorraine, M. J., 14

Los Angeles, CA, 132

Lyle, WA, 127

McKay, Alexander, 38–39

McKay, Margaret Wadine, 41

McKay, Thomas, 39

McKay, William Cameron, 38–9, 41

Mackenzie, Alexander: geographical
    influence of, 82–83, 84, 86

Mackenzie River, 81

Mackie, Richard, 14

McKinney, Sam, 14, 104–5

McLoughlin, John, 41, 102

McNary Lock and Dam, 150

McNickle, D'Arcy, 138

McWhorter, Lucullus, 22

Malaspina, Alejandro, 5

Malick, Abigail: homesteads near Fort
    Vancouver, 10, 114–5, 118, 119, 121–2;
    on flooding Columbia, 87; on
    drowning of son, 114; on Indian
    wars, 116–7; archival letters of, 118;
    on daughter's insanity, 120

Malick, Charles, 115

Malick, Charles ("Little Charlie"), 115,
    118

Malick, George, 114–5

Malick, Hiram, 114, 115

Malick, Jane: youth of, 116, 122; insanity of, 117, 120, 121

Malick, Rachel, 115, 121

Malick, Shindel, 116, 118, 122

Malick, Susan, 118, 122

Malin, James, 135

Martin, Irene, 13

Martin, Kent, 162

Massachusetts, 80

Mazama, Mount, 59

Meinig, Donald W., 85, 139

Melville, Herman, 121

Mencken, Henry Louis, 133

Merriam, H. G., 139

Michilmackinac, MI, 80

Mighetto, Lisa, 13

Miller Island of Columbia River, 21

Mississippi River, 80, 83, 133, 134

Missouri River, 77, 78, 79

Mitchell, John H., 84, 86

Morning Oregonian (Portland): story on first Columbia River centennial, 42–43

Morrison, Toni, 123

Moses Lake, WA, 126

Mulford, Clarence, 132

Mulocks, Ranse, 135

Multnomah (Willamette): and Columbia River myths, 128

Myths, 20–2

National Endowment for the Humanities, 5

Native Americans: as fishers on Columbia River, 4, 8, 11, 19, 140, 145, 160; earliest presence in Columbia Basin, 8; oral literature, place names, knowledge of botanical resources, 8; contacted by explorers, 18–9, 22–3, 106–7; myths associated with, 19–22; and horses, 21–2; learn of white people, 23; smallpox epidemics of, 23–5; assist overland travelers, 113; trade of, 127; portrayed in novels, 128–9. *See also* Rock art; *specific groups*

"Nch'i-Wána" (The Big River). *See* Columbia River

Netboy, Anthony, 4

Nevada, 89

New Deal: constructs dams, 150

New York Public Library, 121

Newburyport, MA, 120

Nez Perce Indians: at Walla Walla Indian Council, 27, 28; in Pacific-Plateau trade network, 77, 78; mentioned, 23, 24

Nisbet, Jack, 14

Nokes, Richard, 14

Nor'Westers. *See* North West Company

Nordquist, Del, 62

North Dakota, 80

North West Company, 37, 38. *See also* Fur trade

Northwest Passage: search for, 79, 80, 81

Northwest Power Planning Council, 145, 163

Ohio River, 83

Okada, John, 138

Okanogan River, 4

Omaha, NE, 120

Orchards, 116, 119, 121–2

Oregon League of Women Voters, 162

Oregon Railway and Navigation Company, 85

Oregon Steam Navigation Company, 90, 148

Oregon Trail. *See* Overland Trail

Ostling, Arlie, 62, 70, 74

"Ouragon River." *See* Columbia River

Overland Astorians. *See* Astorians

Overland Trail: at The Dalles, 10, 155; narratives of, 96, 112; mentioned, 3, 95, 127

Owhi (Yakima), 28

Pacific Fur Company, 37. *See also* Fur trade

Pacific Ocean: exploration of, 5, 81, 95, 106; as route of approach to western America, 95; reached by Lewis and Clark, 95–6

Pacific-Plateau trade system on Columbia River: at The Dalles-Celilo Falls complex, 9, 31, 77, 78, 127; by coastal ships, 23, 37, 50; restricted by Columbia River Bar, 103. *See also* Fur trade; Hudson's Bay Company

Palmer, Joel, 10, 26

Pasco, WA, 130

Peace River, 81

Pelton, Archibald, 93

Pendleton, OR, 43

Pennsylvania, 115, 116, 117

Petersen, Keith, 13

Petite, Aimable, 40

Petroglyphs. *See* Rock art

Pictographs. *See* Rock art

Picture Rocks Bay of Columbia River, 68

Pitzer, Paul, 12

Platte River, 94, 95, 114

Pleistocene floods, 8, 146

Pomeroy, Earl, 139

Pond, Peter, 81, 83

Portland State University, 5

Portland, OR, 118, 121, 130, 139, 148, 153

Potomac River, 83

Powell, John Wesley, 90

Priest Rapids Dam, 60, 62, 64

Priest Rapids Indians, 25

Priest Rapids of Columbia River: as rock art site, 54, 56, 74; mentioned, 18, 32

Puget Sound Power and Light: concern for rock art sites, 71, 73

Puget Sound, 5

Pyle, Robert Michael, 14

Railroads: influence of, 85, 153

Raver, Paul, 149–50

Resolution (sloop-of-war), 81

Ridlington, Sandy, 13

Rio Grande, 89

Ritzville, WA, 126

"River of the West": geographic confusion about, 9, 80, 82; mentioned, 86. *See also* Columbia River

Robbins, Tom, 138

Robbins, William G., 155

Robinson, Marilynne, 138

Rock art: of Columbia River, 8–9; locations of, 54, 56, 62, 64, 66, 74; as historical and cultural record, 56, 60, 75; categories and styles of, 56; interpretation of, 58, 75; dating of, 59–60; documentation of, 62, 64, 73–4; destruction of, 62, 64

Rock Creek Indians, 19

Rock Island Dam, 71

Rock Island Rapids on Columbia River, 54, 56, 59

Rocky Reach Dam, 74

Rogers, Robert, 79–80, 83
Rogue River Indians, 116
"Roll on, Columbia" (song), 85, 86
Ronda, James, 9–10
Roosevelt, WA, 21
Ross, Alexander, 78, 100
Ross, Nancy Wilson, 138
Russell, Charles Marion, 132

Sahaptian: as Native American language
    of, 19, 20, 21; tribal legends of, 22;
    and Pacific-Plateau trade network,
    77; mentioned, 53
Saint Helens, Mount, 23–4
Salem, OR, 121
Salishan: as Native American language,
    19, 20; mentioned, 53
Salmon: influenced by condition of
    Columbia River, 4, 13, 140, 144, 145,
    158–61; literature on, 13; as food, 18,
    115; fishing at Fivemile Rapids, 20;
    mythical stories about, 21; as trade
    item, 49, 77, 106, 107. See also Fish
    runs
San Francisco, CA, 120
Schafer, Joseph, 131
Schlissel, Lillian, 10, 87
Schwantes, Carlos A., 139
Scofield, John, 14
Seattle, 126
Selam, James, 31
Sentinel Bluff , WA, 55, 62, 64
Shaver, Homer, 149
Shoalwater Bay Indians, 43
Shoshoni Indians, 23, 77
Simmer, Harold, 64, 73
Skamakowa, WA, 13
Skilloot Indians, 79
Slacum, William, 95, 103–4

Smallpox, 23–4
Smith, Harlan, 62
Smith, Henry Nash, 132, 141
Smith-Rosenberg, Carroll, 119–20
Smohalla, 25–6, 32
Snake Indians. See Shoshoni Indians
Snake River: dams on, 13, 150, 156, 158;
    sockeye salmon in, 144; mentioned,
    4, 128, 148
Sohappy, David, Sr., 32
Sohappy, Richard, 32
Sohappy v. Smith. See U.S. v. Oregon
South Dakota, 80
Spanish Castle,WA, 55, 70
Spaulding, Henry, 84, 86
Spokane, WA , 126
Spokane Indians, 25
Spokane River, 4
Spokane, Portland, and Seattle Railway,
    85
Stafford, Kim, 13
Steamboats: on Colorado River, 90; on
    Columbia River, 134, 153, 154
Stern, Theodore, 14, 43
Stevens, Isaac I.: conducts treaty coun-
    cils, 26–8; ambiguity of treaties
    written, 29; on Columbia River,
    148–9
Stevens, James, 135
Stilgoe, John, 85
Stockdale, Tom, 68, 70
Stockton, CA, 121
Strong, Ted, 160
Sturgeon: as rock art image, 62
Sutters Mill, CA, 115
Syphilis, 23–24

Tacoma, WA, 130
Tamura, Linda, 14

Taylor, Joseph, 13
Teal, Joseph Nathan, 154–5
Teit, James, 58
Tenino Indians, 78
Teton Sioux Indians, 79
Tewatcon, Susanne, 40
The Dalles, OR: described, 130, 133–4;
    floods at, 151; mentioned, 153.
    See also The Dalles–Celilo Falls
    complex
The Dalles–Celilo Canal, 154–5
The Dalles–Celilo Falls complex: Na-
    tive American trade at, 9, 31, 77–9;
    as indicator of changes on Columbia
    River, 9–10; Oregon Trail at, 10; im-
    portance to Native Americans, 18,
    22; mythical origin of, 21; as slave
    market, 23; and rock art, 56; steam-
    boats at, 90, 153; canal projects at,
    154–5; salmon at, 159–60; drowning
    of, 161; mentioned, 92, 117
The Dalles Dam, 20, 21, 161
Thompson, David: explorations of,
    14; encounters Native Americans,
    18–9, 25; describes rock art site, 71;
    describes Columbia River rapids,
    154–5
Thompson, Jennifer Jeffries, 15
Thorn, Jonathan, 92, 100–1
Tomanawash, Bobby, 60
Tonquin (brig): crosses Columbia River
    Bar, 100–2; mentioned, 10, 39, 92
Toot, Puck Hyat, 62, 75
Tourism, 153
Trade. See Pacific-Plateau trade system
    on Columbia River
Train, George Francis, 159
Tsagiglalal (She Who Watches), 54
Turner, Frederick Jackson, 131

Tute, James, 80
Twain, Mark, 89, 133, 134
Twins: in rock art, 66, 70

Umatilla Indians, 27, 41, 78
Umatilla River, 150
Union Pacific Railroad, 85
U.S.-Canada Columbia River Treaty,
    151–2, 158
U.S. Exploring Expedition. See Wilkes,
    Charles
U.S. v. Oregon: and Indian fishing
    rights, 32
U.S. v. Winans (1905): and Indian
    fishing rights, 31
University of Washington: archaeology
    programs at, 62, 66

Van Doren, Carl, 139
Van Dyke, Henry, 87
Vancouver, George, 5, 81, 95, 106
Vancouver, WA, 5, 121
Vantage, WA: as rock art site, 54, 64, 66,
    68, 70; mentioned, 126
Veterans of Foreign Wars, 119
Victor, Frances Fuller, 11, 131–1, 153
Vietnam War Memorial, 118–9
Villard, Henry, 85

Wagoner, David, 138
Waldo, Harold, 85
Walla Walla, WA, 26
Walla Walla Indian Council (1855),
    27–8
Walula Indians, 78
Wanapam Indians: long-house of,
    32; homelands of, 56, 60; rock art
    of, 74
Wanapum Dam, 70

Wappato, 77
Warren, Robert Penn, 119, 145–6, 163
Wasco Indians, 77
Washington Public Power Supply System, 92
Washington State Historical Society, 5
Washington State Planning Commission: report on Columbia River Gorge, 156–7
Washington State University–Vancouver, 5
Webb, Walter Prescott, 135
Welch, James, 138
Wenatchee, WA, 64, 71, 74, 156
Wenatchee Indians, 56
Wenatchee River, 4
Wheat, 84, 85
Whiskey Dick Canyon, WA, 55, 70
White, Richard: as author, 12; on twentieth-century roles of Columbia River, 140, 147; quoted, 158
Whitman, Marcus, 26, 41
Whitman, Narcissa, 26, 102
Wilbur, James, 32
Wilkes, Charles: exploring expedition of, 25, 39; crosses Columbia River Bar, 95, 97
Willamette Indians, 128
Willamette River, 4, 128, 130
Willamette Valley: glacial erratics in, 8; population growth in, 115
Winther, Oscar Osborn, 136

Winther, Sophus K., 138
Winthrop, WA, 129
Wishram Indians, 77
Wister, 129
Wister, Owen, 129
Women: journals of, 112. See also Malick, Abigail
Wood, Grant, 136
Woodward, C. Van, 119
Woody, Elizabeth, 13
World War II: transforms American West, 137; transforms Columbia River, 149–50
Writers' Conference on the Northwest, 139
Wyden, Ron, 162–3

Yakama Indians: reservation of, 19, 30; treaty of, 26–7; rock art of, 74; and Pacific-Plateau trade network, 78; and salmon, 160
Yakima Polychrome: style of rock art, 56, 68
Yakima River, 4
Yakima Tribe v. Taylor: and Indian fishing rights, 31
Yale University, 118, 122
Yallup, Bill, 161
York River, 83
Young Chief (Cayuse), 28

Zenk, Henry, 9